OUTSIDER

AN OLD MAN, A MOUNTAIN
AND THE SEARCH FOR
A HIDDEN PAST

BRETT POPPLEWELL

HarperCollins*Publishers*Ltd

Outsider
Copyright © 2023 by Brett Popplewell.
All rights reserved.

Published by HarperCollins Publishers Ltd

First published in Canada by Collins in an original trade paperback edition: 2023

This HarperCollins Publishers Ltd mass market edition: 2025

No part of this book may be used or reproduced in any manner whatsoever without written permission.

Without limiting the author's and publisher's exclusive rights, any unauthorized use of this publication to train generative artificial intelligence (AI) technologies is expressly prohibited.

HarperCollins books may be purchased for educational, business or sales promotional use through our Special Markets Department.

HarperCollins Publishers Ltd
Bay Adelaide Centre, East Tower
22 Adelaide Street West, 41st Floor
Toronto, Ontario, Canada
M5H 4E3

www.harpercollins.ca

Library and Archives Canada Cataloguing in Publication is available on request

ISBN 978-1-4434-7661-4

The author would like to acknowledge funding support from the Ontario Arts Council, an agency of the Government of Ontario.

Printed and bound in the United States of America

BVGM 9 8 7 6 5 4 3 2 1

For Marie,
who listened from a hospital bed while I read
through the earliest pages of this text and who
remained with me through the final draft.

ALSO BY BRETT POPPLEWELL

The Escapist:
Cheating Death on the World's Highest Mountains
(with Gabriel Filippi)

CONTENTS

AUTHOR'S NOTE		VII
PROLOGUE		1
CHAPTER 1	*The Man on the Mountain*	12
CHAPTER 2	*The Stories We Tell*	25
CHAPTER 3	*In Dag's Range*	38
CHAPTER 4	*The Death Race*	54
CHAPTER 5	*On Aging*	77
CHAPTER 6	*The Stories We Don't Tell*	88
CHAPTER 7	*Adopted Sins*	107
CHAPTER 8	*Argentina, 1949*	114
CHAPTER 9	*The Long Fall*	123
CHAPTER 10	*Kindred Spirits*	137
CHAPTER 11	*Life on Skis*	151
CHAPTER 12	*Learning to Run*	163

CONTENTS

CHAPTER 13	*Goldfinger*	174
CHAPTER 14	*The World's First Extreme Skier*	197
CHAPTER 15	*Atonement*	215
CHAPTER 16	*Alienated from Birth*	229
CHAPTER 17	*Fortune's Fool*	244
CHAPTER 18	*Descension*	258
CHAPTER 19	*The Psychology of Reinvention*	271
CHAPTER 20	*Never Die Easy*	287
CHAPTER 21	*Hidden in the Past*	300
CHAPTER 22	*A Prodigal Son*	312
CHAPTER 23	*Hedvig's Fate*	326
CHAPTER 24	*All We Leave Behind*	338
CHAPTER 25	*Message in a Bottle*	350
EPILOGUE	*The Last Plateau*	367

ACKNOWLEDGEMENTS 373

AUTHOR'S NOTE

There is pleasure from learning the simple truth, and there is a pleasure from learning that the truth is not simple.

—WAYNE C. BOOTH

Everything that follows is true, or as close to the truth as I could capture. I write these words on a desk cluttered with files and correspondence in multiple languages. Old photographs, newspaper clippings and journals filled with the inner thoughts and methodic scrawl of a complicated hermit litter my desk. The smell of campfire coming out of those journals permeates my office—a reminder that one day, not long ago, an old man entrusted me with the stories of his life and then ran back into the forest. I am neither a detective nor a psychologist, but in the pages that follow I inhabit the role of both. Many of the actors central

AUTHOR'S NOTE

to this book are no longer alive. Some spoke with me at length before they died; others left behind trails of thoughts, memories and important details that I have gathered from interviews with people they confided their stories to and through archival research in Norway, Sweden, Germany and Canada. Conversations and events have been reconstructed from memories, often old and surely faded, simplified and distorted by the lens of time. It is my hope that within this text, undue meaning has not accidentally been assigned to experiences that never had any.

A narrative line has been imposed on the disparate lives of Dag Aabye in the pursuit of cause, effect and, ultimately, understanding of a man who was otherwise misunderstood. Dag is the primary source of much of what follows. Where possible, I have corroborated details of his life with other sources. At times, those sources had different views and interpretations of what happened and why. In cases where Dag's truth differed from others' or my own, I have tried to capture the disparity with fairness and accuracy.

BRETT POPPLEWELL
2023

PROLOGUE

Old people need superheroes too.
—DAG AABYE

The last of the *Übermensch* runs through the night, alone. He carries no identification, but the scars on his face, hands and body tell of an 80-year struggle to survive on the edge of society. He has been starved, abandoned and trapped in a foreign land for nearly 50 years, unable or unwilling to get back to the place that made him. Conceived in war, he is the aged, mangled remnant of a darker time. And yet he is innocent.

There is no light beyond the glow of his headlamp as he races past snow-covered hemlock, fir and pine. The sound of frozen dirt crunching beneath his feet dissipates as he nears the edge of a cliff wall. His are not the only tracks out here, but they are the only sign that a human has been here. He plants his feet in the snow next to the paw prints of a mountain lion that stalks this hillside. He knows she's out there. He has seen her eyes watching from the shadows while he runs. But the innocent mind has no fear. Even when it should.

Fingers gnarled, arms bloodied, shoulder shattered, teeth broken, heels battered—the old man keeps driving his body forward, one boot drop at a time. He reaches out and wraps his clawed hand around the dormant trunk of an aspen and uses it to slingshot his body away from the cliff's edge, and upwards, regaining the mountain lion's trail as he makes for a frozen waterfall that few have ever seen. To those who have seen him, his age, coupled with his tattered boots, gloves and duct-taped jacket, project an image of vulnerability. His face, masked in a frosted beard, is chapped and weathered by decades of cold and sun. Long-haired and scraggly, he looks as ancient as a man would having lived in a school bus parked in a forest since the start of the 21st century. And yet buried within his aging frame is a strength that seems to keep him safe.

He steps onto a snow-covered log that fell over a rushing stream a long time ago. He extends his arms like a tightrope walker and uses the log as a natural bridge. It leads him over the stream and upwards to the source of the rushing water, a 10-metre waterfall that smashes over rocks before freezing along the banks of the stream. He reaches out and touches the cliff wall beside the falls, then marks his time on the watch that has been clocking this run. It has been 48 minutes since he left his camp in the dead of night on a quest for water.

He dips his hand into the runoff, draws it to his face and drinks. Then he turns back toward the camp he has kept hidden from society ever since he decided to disappear into these woods and run, endlessly, both away from, and toward, death.

IN HIS LATER years, whenever he would wander out of his forested lair, run down a winding mountain road and re-enter civilization for food, drink or a phone call, the people who would see him would often stop what they were doing and stare with a mix of bewilderment, pity and awe as he chugged along in his tattered clothing. To those who had never heard of him, he was an odd-looking outcast who smelled of campfire and days-old sweat. But to those aware of his legend, he was a human curio. Later, when he was out of sight, they would tell how they had spotted the mythical mountain man who lived alone out of society's reach. To them, he was like a sasquatch, elusive and wild. Hard to find and even harder to catch, though he moved slowly and had been running in and out of the Okanagan Valley for years.

In the stories often told he had been the greatest skier ever to have lived; a playboy stunt double for James Bond; a nomad and a modern-day Norseman who had travelled the world by land and sea. They said he had leapt from helicopters, triggered avalanches—only to outpace them on skis—and freefallen over cliffs before anyone else did that sort of thing. Once heralded as the world's first extreme skier, he was now among the world's oldest ultramarathon runners, a competitor who raced with a backpack full of boiled potatoes—which he consumed, midrace, for energy—and who possessed a supernatural capacity to push his body further and further as he aged. Some said he wandered into the forest because he lost millions of dollars. Others said he gave the fortune away to pursue a life of solitude, preferring to commune with bears rather than humans.

The stories were all somewhat true, but there were parts of his life that no one could ever fill in, especially the beginning. Those who knew him over the years never really knew where he had come from. He had always been an enigma, even to his family back in Norway. To them he was just a mysterious boy who showed up one day on a farm in the middle of a war. Not even his Canadian ex-wife, who spent more than 20 years trying to understand him, ever felt she knew who he was. He had four children in total, though he knew only three of them and was speaking to only one of them. He was loved by many over the years, but everyone who got close to him ultimately abandoned him or was abandoned by him. He was easy to love, but difficult to live with and even harder to understand. The many twists and turns of his life made his story seem too apocryphal to believe, even to his children. And yet, on some level, he was as natural and authentic as the forest in which he lived.

When confronted with questions about his origin, on those occasions when he would descend from the forest and run into a bar and attract the attention of a curious stranger, the old man would say little, declaring, in a soft, indecipherable European accent: "I was born in captivity. It was nature that set me free."

The truth, however, was far darker than he ever let on.

The full nature of his lineage had been hidden by design, and what little he knew, he rarely discussed. He was the orphan of a distant war whose story traced to the pre-dawn darkness of April 9, 1940—four months before his conception.

THAT APRIL MORNING a thick fog rolled over the North Sea, concealing the masts and periscopes of the German navy cutting through the waves in the night. The future fathers of countless Norwegian-born children were in that fog, creeping toward Norway, along with the massive strength of Adolf Hitler's navy.

To the German soldiers on board those ships, theirs was a noble endeavour, made necessary by British attempts to cut off the Fatherland from the iron ore it required to survive. But to the German commanders directing the invasion from Berlin, the iron ore was just one element of what they wanted out of Norway. They were after Nordic blood. It was the contrived mythological connection between the Third Reich and the Norsemen of old that would eventually lead Heinrich Himmler to follow the soldiers north. As head of the SS, Himmler had developed a twisted yet long-term strategy to increase the German population with what he considered the purest Aryan stock.

Just after four on that April morning, a 64-year-old Norwegian colonel, stationed inside an 85-year-old fortress on the edge of Oslofjord, thought he saw something moving through the searchlights cutting through the fog. The coldest winter in Europe's recorded history had just ended, and Birger Eriksen could still see his breath as he peered out at what he swore was a ship's mast drifting through the night.

Within hours, the Norwegian king and his government had escaped Oslo and headed north. But before the morning was out, Stuka dive-bombers were strafing Oslo while paratroopers dropped from the sky around the city and into the forests and fields beyond. By midafternoon, German soldiers were in the streets while Nazi officers stepped off warships in the harbour. The officers oversaw the deployment of the 10,000 soldiers who were flooding into the city while a further 290,000 eventually took to the hills, fields and fjords that made up the Norwegian countryside.

Outside the capital, Norway quickly became an active war zone as British and French expeditionary forces mobilized into the north of the country and began propping up the besieged kingdom of Haakon VII and his government. For 62 days, the Axis and the Allies led bloody attacks and counterattacks across the Norwegian countryside. Then, on June 7, King Haakon and his only son fled for England. Three days later, what remained of the Norwegian forces capitulated. The complete German occupation of Norway had begun, and as the summer sun cast long shadows over the arctic city, a garrison of 300,000 troops spread out over the land. But it was in Oslo where the main force of the Gestapo, the Nazi secret police, took up headquarters, helping to keep the Norwegian population in line with Nazi doctrine and perpetuating the myth of a centuries-old bond between the Nordic and Germanic peoples.

The effectiveness of the Nazi propaganda machine had convinced members of the SS that it was their civic duty to mate with Nordic women of suitable backgrounds, of which Oslo had plenty. Though the German government officially forbade its soldiers from marrying women in occupied territory, it actively condoned and, indeed, sponsored the impregnation of Norwegian women by SS officers. One SS slogan captured the concept in a single line: "After the victory on the battlefield comes the victory in the cradle." The pairings were as systematic as they were passionate—prospective mothers were screened, their racial purity documented and judged for suitability. But not even the Nazi regime, which was prone to documenting countless aspects of life under their control, could gauge just how many children to expect. The Germans were just six months into the occupation when the prospect of a baby boom was being openly discussed by high-ranking Nazi officials in the aftermath of the invasion. At the centre of the discussions was Heinrich Himmler, whom Hitler appointed to be the Reich Commissar for the Strengthening of German Ethnic Stock.

Part of his mandate was to oversee a program of his own creation: Lebensborn e.V.—"the fountain of life." At its core, the Lebensborn was a state-sanctioned association of Nazi leaders bent on creating a master race and reversing the falling birth rate in Germany.

Supported by the pseudo-science of Nazi eugenics, the Lebensborn aimed to systematically screen young women and lent financial support to those who could bear the children of the SS officers. Himmler wasn't just the most vocal proponent of the program; the entire operation was under his personal direction. Which is partly why, nine months after the invasion, Himmler flew to Norway. That was January 1941, and shortly after he left, 12 Lebensborn centres, including maternity clinics, homes for children and homes for expectant mothers, began appearing in Norway.

More than 700 Norwegian babies were officially born into the Lebensborn that year, the first of an estimated 8,000 children registered in the program. There were 4,000 more Norwegian babies born to German soldiers before the war was through. Some were the product of rape, others were born from short-lived affairs. Many were adopted by sympathetic families. Sometimes the father's name was altered on or omitted from the child's birth or baptismal certificate. Sometimes the omission was for the protection of the children themselves. Other times it was for the mothers. Norway may have been a conquered state, but sleeping with the enemy was still a crime in the eyes of the Resistance. The women were protected by, and paid a stipend by, the Lebensborn, which put them up in commandeered well-appointed hotels where the mothers could be shielded from the ire of Norwegian society. But when their children were born, the needs of the mothers became secondary to the needs of the children. Collusion and propaganda set in, and the mothers, who were often alone, having been isolated from and ostracized by family and society, were led to give up their children for the betterment of the Reich. Most of the mothers chose to nurse their babies to the healthy age of one, while struggling not to forge too strong a bond with a child they were destined to lose. Roughly 250 children, deemed to be the "purest of the pure," were sent to Germany. Those children deemed of the next best stock were placed with suitable Norwegian families allied to the German cause. Others remained in a state-sanctioned purgatory, forced to ride out the war from the confines of an orphanage.

On May 15, 1941, a blond-haired, blue-eyed boy was born to an unwed mother living in an

Oslo hotel. His name was Erik. For the earliest days of the boy's life, he lived with his mother in an apartment in a part of the city that had become the epicentre of the Nazi Party's Norwegian rule. One day, before he was seven months old, the boy's mother bundled him up and took him to an orphanage next to a prison where enemies of the occupation were tortured and murdered. She passed uniformed soldiers in the street as she pushed her way toward the orphanage. Then she left him there.

The search began for new parents and a new name.

ONE

THE MAN ON THE MOUNTAIN

Time matters most when time is running out.
—DAG AABYE

How deeply time defines us.

I was a 32-year-old workaholic when I became puzzled and inspired by a mysterious senior citizen who lived on a mountain and was pushing the limits of the human mind and body. I was a full-time magazine writer, happily married, living the urban millennial dream in downtown Toronto. I defined myself, as many young journalists do, by the stories I told, convinced the words I wrote mattered as much as anything else I did in my life. The people I wrote about were always different, but my approach was generally the same: plant myself into the lives of others and shadow them until I "figured them out." Only when my notebooks were full would I announce my departure. I would wave goodbye and head back home to my desk where, surrounded by notes and listening to their voices coming out of my recorder, I would graft their projection into a Word document on my computer. I never meant for anything I did in journalism to feel transactional, and yet it was. When it was all said and done and my words were finally in print, I would move on. Find another story. Another subject. Another person.

Then I met Dag Aabye.

It was journalistic curiosity that first led me to fly across three time zones in search of a man who lived in a school bus on the side of a mountain and whose name I had no idea how to pronounce. I never fathomed then that my initial encounter with the Okanagan's enigmatic old trail runner would launch a six-year quest that would take me back to that mountainside countless times as I tried to help him figure out who he was and explain to others why he was the way he was. Or that along the way he would help me understand myself and show me why I am the way I am.

But before any of that, I sat in a Vietnamese restaurant in Toronto listening to vague, incomplete and somewhat incomprehensible portions of the legend of Dag Aabye, which had found their way to me via a photo editor named Myles McCutcheon. Myles was a CrossFit enthusiast and a trail runner, and a former colleague from my time working at a sports magazine. Having spent a lot of time around professional athletes, he wasn't enamoured with fame and celebrity culture. But he had been transfixed by a white-haired "Jesus figure" he had seen six years earlier at the top of a jagged, desolate mountain, 75 kilometres into a 125-kilometre ultramarathon. Dag had been lodged in Myles's mind since that day, and by the fall of 2015, Myles was eager to lodge him into mine.

"Why is this guy so special?" I asked.

He described Dag as a reclusive superathlete who spent his days training on hand-cut trails no one else knew existed.

"He's like Superman or Tarzan, if Superman or Tarzan ever grew old and lived in a bus," Myles said.

"Superman was an orphaned alien," I said.

"Exactly."

"And Tarzan was a feral child who became a feral man."

"You're getting it."

I was intrigued. I tried to visualize the character Myles was describing, right down to the school bus parked in the wild. "This guy sounds like another Chris McCandless type," I said.

It was impossible not to think of McCandless, the young man who was immortalized in Jon Krakauer's *Into the Wild*. In 1992, McCandless had run away from his well-off family and hitchhiked to Alaska, then walked into the wilderness to live and ultimately die in a Fairbanks city bus. I appreciated the McCandless story for the tragic romance of an ideological young man who tried to live entirely detached from the grid. But like many who read Krakauer's book, I believed McCandless had died as a result of his own naivety.

"No," Myles assured me. "He's way deeper. McCandless was a young innocent. Dag is the old guru."

Myles explained that long before Dag became a trail runner he had been an actor and a stuntman with several bit parts in blockbuster films in the UK. After he came to Canada in the mid-1960s he quickly became known as the world's first extreme skier. Then he threw away fame and wandered into the forest, where he stayed, only to emerge, years later, as one of the world's oldest long-distance runners.

The more Myles spoke, the more Dag began to

personify a Forrest Gump–like character. Pierre Trudeau, the Beatles, Ursula Andress, Michael Caine—Dag had a connection to all of them. But to Myles, Dag represented something more primal. His lifestyle made him a case study to support a theory that human beings had evolved to run extreme long distances, farther than any other creature on earth, but that society had altered our evolution and made us sedentary.

It was a theory that emerged in 2004 in the academic writings of evolutionary biologist Daniel Lieberman and biologist Dennis Bramble and was later popularized in *Born to Run*, a book by Christopher McDougall, who spent time living in Mexico among a reclusive tribe of aboriginal superathletes known as the Tarahumara ("those who run fast"). Renowned for being the world's best ultrarunners, the Tarahumara have been known to run 320 kilometres in sandals while avoiding many of the common injuries faced by runners. Myles was a proponent of the "endurance running hypothesis," which argues that humans are able to run extreme long distances because of evolutionary adaptations that helped us travel between villages, outrun prey and scavenge for meat in a timely manner. But contemporary behaviours have moved us away from this ability. The very structure of our feet and the way we plant them on this earth has been altered by footwear, encouraging injuries, while our need to run long distances has been eliminated by the luxuries of modern science and society.

Dag, on the other hand, lived in the wild and trained his body to run for up to 24 hours straight. Though he did not hunt or scavenge for food, he was living largely outside society, running to live and living to run—1,200 hours a year. Myles wanted to capture his story on camera, but he needed a writer. That's where I came in.

"He literally runs 125 kilometres straight?" I asked.

"Yes," Myles said.

"Against people a quarter his age?"

"That's right."

There was something about an old man challenging our societal understanding of aging and athleticism that piqued my interest. I was fascinated by the notion that a vagabond superathlete appeared to be aging slower than the rest of us while also adhering to a simple life in the wild. As a reporter, I search for people with interesting stories to tell. I worked as an investigative journalist with the *Toronto Star*, where I exhausted my late 20s exposing con artists and thieves, examining the way humans tended to bend the rules that regulate our society in order to advance themselves at the expense of others. But it wasn't until I joined *Sportsnet* magazine that I gravitated toward stories about people who, either by nurture or nature, had become supremely gifted at one thing in life, often to the detriment of other aspects of their existence.

It didn't matter whether I was writing about a rising talent in hockey, baseball or even chess; the tension was in how far they could push themselves, physically, emotionally and mentally, before hitting their peak. I found mid-career athletes more interesting because they had a fuller appreciation of how quickly people begin to fade. But it was the older, broken-down athletes who understood, better than anyone else I had ever spoken to, the full emotional toll of human decline. They were the ones who were able to describe the inevitable tragedy that befalls every athlete after they reach the point where they can no longer do what they once could.

It seemed this man Myles had met on a mountaintop was doing more to push beyond the limits of the human body than any other athlete I had met or written about.

The only question I had was whether Myles actually knew enough about Dag to find him again. "It seems pointless to jump on a plane, fly across the country and comb the forest looking for a guy who prefers to be hidden," I said. "Do you know where his school bus is parked?"

Myles shook his head. "Here's the thing," he

replied. "There's this sports bar in Vernon where he likes to drink." Myles had been leaving messages at the bar for weeks. He still hadn't received a response from Dag, but he wanted to be ready to fly in the event that Dag ever called him back. A few months passed before Myles and I reconnected about the project. By that time Myles was starting to get calls from payphones across the Okanagan Valley. "The other day I got this call from Armstrong, BC," Myles said. "I picked it up and it was Dag. I explained to him who I was and that I wanted to shoot a film about him in the wild. He said we could follow him. All we have to do is make sure we're in a sports pub on the other side of the country on a Thursday one month from now at 11 a.m. I think if we don't show up we probably won't hear from him again."

"What do we do if *he* doesn't show up?" I asked.

Myles looked at me blankly for a moment, then said: "Then we'll have to go for a long walk through the woods."

A MONTH LATER, I sat inside Pearson International Airport, waiting for my plane to arrive. I was carrying a duffel bag stuffed with printouts of every news story and online post I could find about Dag. Over the course of two plane rides and seven hours, I consumed all of it. There were lots of stories, but few tangible details. Elements of his life had been published in magazines and newspapers, and in books about the history of modern-day skiing. The stories all tended to breeze over the more complex and misunderstood intricacies of his life—like why he wandered into the wild or how he became a competitive ultramarathon runner. There were occasional mentions of family, but never any indication of what they meant to him or what he meant to them. In these stories he simply emerged into the cultural narrative in the mid-1960s as a Hollywood stuntman who had made his name on skis at a time when skiing was beginning to explode as a mass-market sport. Then he disappeared, only to resurface years later as an ultramarathon runner right at the moment that ultrarunning began to take off around the world.

In most of the stories he was described as a hermit. But Dag didn't fit the hermit mould. He would push himself as far from society as he could go, living alone in the wild for weeks with no human contact, then he would return to civilization in search of more than just sustenance. He usually seemed to end up inside a grungy sports bar attached to a gym, where patrons sat under autographed posters of Michael Jordan and Wayne Gretzky, downing beer and chomping on french fries. It was there that Myles had left a note with the bartender. And it was there, in that bar, on November 19, 2015, that I first met Dag Aabye.

THE PUB WAS only a quarter full, but those present were mostly regulars who gathered to drink the afternoon away. I had barely stepped inside when a man on his way out took one look at my peacoat and concluded that I wasn't from anywhere nearby.

"You must be looking for Dag," he said.

"Is he here?" I asked.

The man pointed at a pair of antique Nordic skis that hung on the wall next to the door above a portrait of a young skier jumping off the roof of a hotel circa 1965. I looked closely at the picture.

"He looks a bit different now," the man said. "But you can't miss him." He pushed out of the bar and into the sunlight, and I continued my way inside, toward the sound of Lynyrd Skynyrd.

Dag sat on a bar stool, his back straight as a pencil, a Kokanee beer in one hand and a half-eaten club sandwich in the other. Myles had come in on an earlier flight and rendezvoused with BC-based filmmaker Derek Frankowski. Derek was in his late 30s and had made his name with independent mountain-bike movies and BBC nature films. Myles and Derek stayed on their stools as I approached their table. Dag saw me coming and put down his sandwich, rose to his feet and stood, chest out with his arms at his side, like a soldier at attention. He stood over six feet tall, and though he hadn't weighed himself in 60 years he looked like 140 pounds. His white hair was matted and wild. His nose was long and sharp, his mouth hidden beneath his moustache and beard, which were both the colour of snow. He wore a camouflage-patterned fleece, running pants and boots with duct tape on the inside ankle. He extended his hand. His fingers were curled and bent and his nails were squished, broken or missing after years of neglect and abuse. We shook hands.

"This is Dag," Myles said.

Back where Dag was from people pronounced it "Dog," but ever since he arrived in North America in the mid-1960s, everyone had been calling him "Dayg." His last name was even harder for people to get right. He tended to spell it Aabye, though the proper way, using Norwegian lettering, is Åbye. Both spellings had a way of stumping anyone unfamiliar with Scandinavian languages. He rarely corrected strangers when they struggled to say his name, unless they asked, in which case he would tell them that it was pronounced "Obi, like Obi-Wan Kenobi."

Dag looked at me. "So you're the one who is going to Everest?"

I wasn't sure what Myles had told him.

Dag continued. "I have read that the path to the top is lined with dead bodies, but is it true that the trail to the base is covered with garbage?"

I looked at Myles, unsure where this was going. Myles shrugged. I had been working on a book about a mountain climber from Montreal who had narrowly escaped death on several of the world's highest mountains. And I was preparing for a trip to Nepal, where I hoped to study the psychology of the men and women whose chosen pastime involved dragging their bodies to a place on earth where their blood would turn to sludge, their brains swell, their lungs fill with fluid and their hearts slip into congestive failure.

"I'm not sure about the garbage," I said, "But you're right about the bodies."

"Do you think there's plastic at the top of the mountain?"

I knew there were flags and flag poles up there and discarded oxygen tanks. I hadn't thought about plastic itself. "There probably is," I said.

"Then it's everywhere now." He continued as he reached for his beer. "They say there will soon be more plastic than fish in the oceans."

"I didn't know that," I said.

Myles jumped in and asked Dag if he could take us to his bus. Dag shook his head. Then Myles asked if he could take us out on his trails. It was possible, Dag said, but we would need to be prepared to camp out in the cold. Myles looked at my peacoat and sighed. "We can get ourselves ready," he said.

"Okay then," Dag said. "Tomorrow, I can take you to my training ground."

"Is it far from here?" Myles asked.

"It's a bit of a hike," Dag said.

"What's up there?" Myles asked.

"Twenty-six kilometres of hidden trails," Dag said.

"Hidden?" Myles asked. "Has no one else ever been up there?"

Dag's beard moved along with his lips. "No one else has ever asked."

TWO

THE STORIES WE TELL

*A tale is but half told when
only one person tells it.*
—THE TALE OF GRETTIR THE
STRONG, ICELANDIC SAGA

It was cold and quiet and just after dawn, the temperature slowly creeping above freezing as the sun worked its way over the mountains. Dag sat in the passenger seat of Derek's Subaru, guiding us north through the Okanagan Valley toward an unmarked exit where we would begin our ascent to Dag's camp. The path through the bush was purposely gruelling and uninviting, the entry point so well hidden that even he sometimes struggled to find where it began. Yet it had always been there. He had repurposed an old deer trail used by white-tails, coyotes, bears, wolves and cougars—a natural thoroughfare that led from the scarred tracts of a gravel pit over a stream and up a mountain into the BC backcountry.

Dag directed us to turn off the highway and onto a gravel access road. Up ahead, a smouldering of bones and brush—roadkill and debris that highway workers threw into a heap a few hundred metres from the highway—burned in a bonfire the size of a city bus, just out of view from the transport trucks and day trippers cutting north–south through the frost-covered vineyards and cherry orchards that make up the Okanagan Valley. We weren't more than 50 metres from the highway when he said we would have to proceed the rest of the way on foot. "You'll want to pull your car up next to the bush here," he said. "It will be fine for as long as we're gone."

Derek parked the car out of sight but still near to the main road. Our footsteps crunched in the frosted dirt as we gathered our gear and headed out from the road, following Dag as he navigated around a quarry toward the smoke cloud billowing out of the bonfire. He walked ahead of us, carrying a chainsaw on the end of a stick that he balanced on his shoulder. The chainsaw was a replacement for one at his training camp, which had recently been mauled and dragged through the forest by a bear that had wandered through in search of food.

"You wouldn't believe the damage that one curious bear can do," he said.

We passed the bonfire and trekked beyond the gravel pits through a tall grass field littered with sun-baked rib cages, spinal columns and animal skulls—casualties of human forays into these parts. "This is a sight most people don't like to see," Dag said. The animals were roadkill that had been brought to this place to rot. He stopped beside the carcass of a freshly killed elk, its body broken by a collision on the road, then dumped here for its flesh to be torn to pieces by vultures. Maggots and flies worked through what remained of the meat, consuming everything but the scent of death. That putrid smell, coupled with the killing field itself, seemed the perfect human deterrent, a natural barrier that only the morbidly curious would ever cross.

Dag stepped around the carcass and made his way toward an old barbed wire fence. He gently lowered the chainsaw through to the other side. Then, like a boxer entering a ring, he pushed the wires apart with his hands, careful not to touch the sharp tied barbs. Then he bent his frame, lifted his leg slowly over the barbs, and manoeuvred his way through. Once on the other side he

The path to Dag's training camp began near a burning pile of animal carcasses. (Courtesy of Derek Frankowski)

started the stopwatch on his wrist and waited for the rest of us to get through the fence ourselves.

For another 10 minutes we continued our way up a mud road that had frozen in the night. Then Dag stopped mid-step.

"There's the door," he said. He stepped off the road at an almost indiscernible indent in the frozen ivy that led through a wall of wild larch, pushed the twigs and branches away from his face and disappeared behind the brush. Myles, Derek and I looked at each other briefly. We were each saddled with camera gear as well as the necessities we believed we needed to spend a night in Dag's world: sleeping bags, a tent, food and jugs of water. We tightened the packs on our shoulders, then followed Dag through the twigs and branches and into the forest. Dag travelled light. Other than the chainsaw, he carried only a small backpack. Shortly after veering onto the deer trail, we came upon a fast-moving stream that flowed over our path. A fleece sweater hung from a broken branch next to the stream.

"Is that yours?" I asked.

"Clean laundry," Dag replied.

He reached for the sweater and felt that it was dry. Then he took off his backpack and placed the sweater inside next to a can of beans, a box of matches and some bread he had picked up the previous day while in town.

"Are we getting close?" I asked. About half an hour had passed since we left the road.

"This is just the start of the trail," Dag replied.

For the next hour we lugged ourselves up a steep incline, grasping for support from the thin trunks of the trees that grew out of the hillside as we made our way along a series of switchbacks that took us upwards to an old logging road, which Dag told us had been used by horses and abandoned 80 years earlier. The road had been grown over by 50-year-old seedlings that had sprouted from the overhanging branches of the spruce and pine that were planted after the first loggers came here and ripped out the old-growth forests to build masts and homes and tables and chairs. Myles, Derek and I stopped and leaned against a downed log to catch our breath and drink some water. Dag drank nothing. Then we continued up the old logging road to its end before veering onto another deer trail, continuing our climb while gaining 335 metres of elevation over an eight-kilometre hike.

It was late morning when Dag finally stopped and told us there was something he wanted us to see. He walked us to the ledge of a high cliff wall. The tops of 30-metre spruce trees sprawled beneath us, stretching into the Okanagan Valley, which rambled on toward the southern horizon. But for the smokestacks spewing nitrogen oxide, sulphur and carbon out of the city in the distance, the scene could have been a Bob Ross painting.

"This is my windowless view of society," he said. There were thousands of people in the valley below. None could see what he saw.

He turned from the ledge and carried on up the hill. We had been trekking for the better part of the morning, and the first sign that we were nearing Dag's actual training ground came when he reached for his wrist to press his stopwatch again. He had been timing his ascent. It was how he gauged his pace and the only way to know whether he was moving any faster than he had the last time he trekked to this camp, or the time before that.

He took a mental note of the time on his watch, then looked at the thin layer of snow beneath his feet. "When there's more snow I make dummy tracks around here, just in case anyone finds my trail," he said.

"Have you ever seen anyone else up here?" Derek asked.

"I don't think anyone's been up here since the loggers left," he said. "When I find bear droppings on my trail I get excited. If I ever saw garbage I'd get scared. Then I'd know I'd been found."

"Are there many bears up here?" I asked.

"They're all through here," Dag said. "But they should be hibernating by now. I don't set out looking for them. A black bear came to visit me a couple of weeks ago at my bus. It was five in the morning. He was trying to break into my food storage. He woke me up."

"Jesus," I said.

"I keep my food in a cold box chained to the front of my bus," Dag explained. "I could hear him trying to pull it away. The whole bus was moving, so I went outside to talk to him."

I thought he was joking, until it became clear that he wasn't.

"How do you talk to a bear?" I asked.

"You say, 'Hey bear, hey, hey bear. That's my food, bear.'"

"And what did the bear do?" I wondered.

"The bear did what bears do. He stood on his hind legs and got really tall and really loud. They just try to intimidate you, but they don't intimidate me."

I waited, unsure what to make of his story.

Dag pointed to a natural wall of wild incense cedars about 20 metres away. The trees were skinny and young, their branches so intertwined that I couldn't see through to the other side. "My camp is just behind those trees," he said.

He guided us off the main trail and onto a concealed pathway that cut through the cedars. The final stretch of trail was a naturally walled corridor that led to an opening shielded by hills on three sides and thick brush of more cedars mixed with mature hemlock. All of it served to keep Dag's campsite hidden from sight until we were actually standing in it. I was only a metre or so away from his firepit, a simple hole dug into the earth and braced by rocks, when I realized we had arrived. A cast-iron griddle rested by my foot under a centimetre of snow. A camouflage tarp covered Dag's tent, which was actually a portable shed that he bought from a hardware store and carried into the bush five years earlier. He had placed it next to a bench he carved out of a tree trunk and propped up with two wooden stumps. There were other stumps too that served as his furnishings—a stump for eating, a stump for sitting, a stump for cutting wood. When I looked back at the path into Dag's camp I realized I had walked right past a meticulously kept woodpile, chopped and stacked two metres high and wedged between the trunks of two great hemlocks.

"Welcome to my training camp," Dag said, motioning to the stumps and the bench. "What's mine is yours." He paused. "Though most of this really belongs to nature."

The signs of the bear attack revealed themselves slowly—a shattered coffee cup, the mangled chainsaw, tooth and claw marks on a plastic orange juice container. Dag went over to his tent and unzipped the outer tarp that protected it from the rain. He pulled out a propane stove and some lanterns. Then he dropped his backpack inside on a nest of blankets, sleeping bags and pillows that kept him warm on cold autumn nights. It was November 20, and though he wasn't ready to abandon the camp for the winter, he knew any day the snow would start accumulating, and when that happened it would be too difficult for anyone to get in and out of this site. Then he would retreat to his bus, which served as his primary residence through the long winter months. But he preferred the tranquility and the solitude at his training ground over the tranquility and solitude at his bus, which was comparatively accessible, roughly a 500-metre trek from the nearest gravel road.

"Up here," he explained, "I'm a free man. I can run for days without any distraction. But there's a limit to how long anyone should spend entirely alone." He said he tried to limit his periods of isolation to a maximum of two weeks at a time. "I've gone longer, but it does something to you. It changes the way you think. We are social creatures, herd animals. I crave solitude, but it's not in our nature to be completely cut off from one another."

We had been at the camp only a few minutes, but already the cold was setting in. "We should keep ourselves moving," Dag said. He led us out of the camp and up toward an eagle's perch a few storeys above his camp, where he liked to sit in the sun and record his thoughts in his journal as hawks circled in the sky above. He would watch them dive into the forest. Often they emerged with something squirming in their talons. Sometimes, if he sat really still, a hawk would land close enough for him to watch as it tore its beak through the flesh of its prey.

We were halfway back to his camp when we came across the recent paw prints of a rather large animal.

"What are these from?" I asked.

Dag placed his foot next to the print. "These are too big for a lynx," he said. "I'd say they are from a cougar."

I didn't know much about cougars, but I knew that they liked to ambush their prey.

"How fresh are they?" I asked.

He looked at them again. "Fresher than the snow," he said. Then he looked at me and smiled.

I asked him, "Does it scare you knowing there's a cougar in the area?"

His eyes followed the cougar's track into the bush. Suddenly he was recounting how one night, while trying to run down to the road to escape an impending storm, he could feel that he was being stalked. He could hear something running in the brush beside him. Then he saw it. "I could see its eyes glowing in the dark," he said. "Following me on the trail in the night. You can't give in to fear. If you're scared, you lose control of yourself. You have to stay in control of yourself. Ultimately, it's the only thing you can actually control."

Night was falling and the temperature had dropped back below freezing by the time we got back to his camp. Dag grabbed some split wood and placed it in the firepit. Then he pulled out a small container of gasoline, poured it onto the wood and struck a match. The fire ignited with a *whoosh*. We warmed our hands as he boiled some water, the remoteness of our surroundings amplified as the darkness set in. The sky was clear, the winds calm. The only source of noise on the entire mountainside: the crackling fire and the steam slowly rising out of the kettle.

Dag poked the fire. "It's important to maintain a link to the world," he said. "Especially when you live the way I do."

It struck me as a perplexing comment from an isolated man.

The kettle whistled and Dag continued talking as he took it off the fire. He was no stranger to solitude, he said, and grew up in a house so big that it had twelve wood stoves. He said his earliest memories were of stoking the fire in his room for hours while committing the Icelandic sagas to memory. He liked the way the stories merged history and fantasy. "Our histories are our own fantasies," he said. "That's memory for you."

He said his father had been a farmer in a valley a few hours northwest of Oslo, where the farms were more or less forests and so his father was also a woodsman who would cut trees only to plant new ones for Dag to inherit. "I grew up wandering that forest," he said. "The trees were young, but the forest was ancient." Growing up, he was told, just as other children were, that thousands of years earlier, Thor and Odin would meet in the forests and fields of Dag's childhood.

The farm of Dag's youth traced back to the Norsemen and still carried the Norse name of Hovlandsmoen, which roughly translated means an elevated flat land, though the etymology from the old texts linked it to a place of worship for the Norse gods. It was all just Nordic myth, of course, but it was local legend ingrained in the land and the people who lived there. Dag described days spent running through the woods, digging for Viking treasures, searching for Nordic trolls and pretending he was Thor. It was escapism for a boy growing up surrounded by war. He wasn't yet four when his father took him out into the field, loaded a rifle, placed it in his hands and taught him how to line the sights and squeeze the trigger. He was also trained when to run and where to hide when the soldiers came.

"If the phone rang only twice, that was the sign," he said. "That's how we knew. It didn't matter where you were or what you were doing. There was always a packed bag waiting by the door. I don't remember much from the war, but I do remember that."

The night was getting colder now. He fetched another log and threw it on the fire, and we watched as the flames grew while the moonlight cut through the trees.

"No life is perfect," Dag said. "Only moments are." His grandmother had once told him that.

THREE

IN DAG'S RANGE

Caminante, no hay camino.
Se hace el camino al andar.

(Traveller, there is no path.
The path is made by walking.)

—ANTONIO MACHADO, QUOTED IN DAG'S JOURNALS

I awoke to the sound of rustling outside my tent. The forest and sky were still cast in black, but Dag was up, stoking the fire and restless. I rolled over in my sleeping bag and checked my iPhone. It was almost dead and out of reception, but still useful as a clock. It was nearly 5 a.m.

This was often the time Dag got up to run. I hadn't thought about what his world must have looked like in the dead of night until I was lying in my sleeping bag, exhausted and cold. In that moment I simultaneously appreciated and loathed whatever it was that gave the old man his energy.

His footsteps crunched in the snow. Then came the sound of an axe splitting fresh logs for the fire. I tried to steal another minute of sleep and was just starting to drift off when Dag turned on his portable radio and began listening to the news. It was the top of the hour and the airwaves circled the country, carrying reports of power, celebrity and catastrophe to distant ears—including the hermitic man living on the edge of nowhere. Reports of a recent election in Argentina mixed with details of a terrorist attack in Tunisia and a new study warning that more than half the trees in the Amazon were at risk of extinction.

I pawed around my tent searching for a headlamp. I turned it on and strapped it to my forehead. Suddenly I could see the hoarfrost on the canvas above. It was well below freezing.

Dag lived for this time of night, the fleeting pre-dawn hours before the day is born, when the nocturnal creatures pass their realm to the diurnal world. Dag sat by the fire, breathing in the cold night air while digesting morsels of the world's problems and recording them in his journal—the election, the terrorist attack and humanity's desecration of the rainforest. I didn't yet understand just how much it all resonated with him. I didn't yet understand much about him, really.

I unzipped my tent and climbed out into the snow. The moonlight cast long shadows over the camp, but the stillness in the dark played tricks on the mind. As did the wind whispering through the cedars. I stretched out my back, looking at nothing yet seeing things in the shadows. The forest had a way of concealing the unknown. And it was the unknown that unnerved me. I turned toward the crackling fire. There was Dag, his face alight, a pen in one hand, his journal in the other. He was wearing reading glasses—the $10 type you pick up at Walmart. He had begun wearing them in his 40s and three decades later still didn't bother with an actual prescription. A kettle rested in the fire by his feet. He was brewing coffee before his run.

I warmed my hands by the fire and asked if he had slept well.

"I've never had trouble sleeping," he said. "But I don't sleep the day away either."

The embers popped and glowed as Myles and Derek joined us by the fire. None of us said anything, leaving the radio to fill the space between us. Dag may have been living on the outskirts of society, but he did better than the three of us at keeping up with what was going on in the world.

He closed his journal, pulled the kettle from the fire and poured four cups of instant coffee, emptying the dregs into a "Rebel Without a Cause" mug that he kept dangling from a nail hammered into a nearby tree. Then he sat back down and listened to the radio.

"A person cannot exist entirely on their own," he said. "They can for a while, but not for long." He had learned that from Henry David Thoreau, one of history's more famous loners. In 1845, Thoreau wandered into a forest hoping to find meaning through a simple, self-sufficient life alone with nature. He wrote about it nine years later in *Walden; or, Life in the Woods*, a book that established the philosophical foundation that inspired generations of romantic recluses to disappear into the woods in search of their own Walden. I have never read *Walden*. Dag, however, knew it well. "If a man does not keep pace with his companions, perhaps it is because he hears a different drummer," Thoreau wrote. "Let him step to the music which he hears, however measured or far away." Thoreau lasted two years, two months and two days in a cabin near Walden Pond in Massachusetts. Dag had been living a life of relative seclusion, either in his bus or at this mountainside camp, for 15 years. But he knew, just as Thoreau did, that to exist alone in nature required one to coexist with society.

Thoreau was rarely "alone" for more than a few weeks at a time. Dag understood why. Like Thoreau, Dag kept himself lucid by pouring his thoughts into his journals. Dag had read *Walden* three times in his life. The first time, he was just a boy at Hovlandsmoen. The second time, he was in his 20s and living in Chile, having wandered there with nothing more than a backpack and skis. The third time, he was living in his bus. Although *Walden* resonated with Dag at a young age, it wasn't until his late 50s that he began living a Thoreauvian existence. Alone in the forest, he surrounded himself now with countless other books he had carried up the mountainside. Dozens of books littered his tent and spilled out into the frost-covered twigs and pine needles that lined his camp. His reading material was as dense as it was informative. Pages of the *New York Times* Sunday edition rested under a tattered, coverless copy of John le Carré's *Tinker, Tailor, Soldier, Spy* and a paperback edition of Charles Dickens's *Great Expectations*, which had been cut in half for portability. There were other books too, with passages cut out because they meant something to him. He would carefully tape the passages into his journal and then write around them, mixing his thoughts with those of others.

"It isn't easy," he said, "to describe what happens to the mind when it's completely cut off from the world outside." That's why he listened to the news. But doing so also served as a way of reminding him why he had trekked into the forest in the first place.

"When I feel like I'm starting to get weird up here," he said, "I run down to the highway and I take a bus into the city. Then I stop in at a McDonald's and I order a sandwich and I sit down and I see these people, all these people, and none of them are talking to each other. They just stare at their phones." He looked at me for confirmation. "Is that how people live now?"

I nodded.

He shook his head. "I have no problem with society. I just don't want to be part of it."

He finished his coffee and rose from the fire, then strapped a headlamp around his tuque, ready to set out on his morning run. It was nearly six and he had a destination in mind, a waterfall, that he preferred to reach in the dark. "It's a 30-minute run if I'm making good time," he said. "Over the ridge and then down a steep gully." He said the falls fed into a stream that was the nearest source of water. I couldn't understand why anyone would purposely set up a camp so far away from the nearest water supply. Dag explained: "If you set your life up so that everything is comfortable, then you never have to work for anything. If you never have to work for anything, then you start to grow old. Most people don't understand that." He said he had constructed his life in order to challenge himself physically and psychologically.

"If we time the journey right," he added, "the view on the way back is as special as anything you've ever seen." He pointed east into the darkness. "The sun will rise over that hill in two hours. When it does, a red sky will filter through the trees like light through stained glass in a cathedral."

He grabbed two collapsible hiking sticks and took a glance at the firepit to make sure it would stay alight but not spread while he was out on his run. Then he turned on his headlamp and headed out into the night beyond his camp. Derek mounted his camera over his shoulders and followed closely behind, trying to capture the essence of a senior citizen running through the wild in the dead of night. Myles ran behind Derek, while I trailed with a notebook. Every so often I would get close enough to hear a gentle, melodic humming as Dag rounded roots and trees, scaling logs and reaching for trunks to help pull himself up an incline or steady his pace on a roughshod descent. It took a while to discern that he was humming the melody from "As Time Goes By." *Dah-dai-dah-dai-dah-dum, dah-dai-dah-dee-dah-dum.*

For 15 minutes we carried on in this way until he crested the ridge. We followed as he ran along the ledge of a cliff with only a few metres of artificial light between himself and a perilous drop. Dag continued upwards along the ledge until he ducked back into the forest toward another deer trail leading into the gully. He slowed his movements as he started to descend toward the sound of water flowing along the gully floor. It was the runoff from the waterfall. The trail into the gully was rugged and steep. Derek turned off his camera and packed it away, not wanting to damage it in a fall. I stuck close to Dag. He seemed vulnerable now, grasping at tree trunks to break his momentum as he descended the frozen terrain. He looked back and noticed I was falling behind. He watched me for a few steps. I clung to a low-hanging branch as I slid to a stop beside him.

"Are you good?" he asked.

"Good," I replied.

"Every footstep matters," he said.

I stood and observed as he continued down into

the gully, nervously watching as his feet slipped out from under him, sliding on a combination of snow and mud. Dag reacted instinctively, jutting his arms back to brace himself against the hill as he fell backwards. His weight was now on his hands, extended behind him, and his feet beneath as he continued his descent. He slid a little farther, then pushed himself upright with his arms and grabbed hold of a well-positioned spruce, stopping himself from a potentially catastrophic injury. The precariousness of Dag's life was on full display. He was 74, an age when a simple slip or a fall can be life-altering. Yet here he was, navigating a dark hillside on a 30-minute search for his version of a faucet.

Undaunted, Dag continued down toward the gully. The snow was thicker there, and the ground was covered in large rocks, many of them coated with ice from the splashing water flowing down the stream. Dag negotiated the rocks as he ran upstream, crisscrossing the water over natural bridges formed by the trunks of trees that had fallen into the gully over decades. It was still dark when we reached the waterfall. The falls were at least 10 metres high. We watched from a distance as the water poured down from above, flickering in the light of our headlamps as it shot over the ice-covered rocks that hung above him.

He waved us forward and explained that he

Dag crossing a log bridge on a pre-dawn run to the hidden waterfall near his training camp. (Courtesy of the author)

didn't believe anyone else alive knew the falls were here. He wasn't convinced that the loggers who had worked in the area years earlier had explored the gully. "The only way to get here is the way we just came," he said. "And I don't think anyone other than me has come that way in years."

We filled our jugs and for a while admired the water cascading over the falls and crystallizing on the rocks below. Then Dag recommended we get moving if we wanted to catch the dawn. We returned to Dag's camp by the same trail, stopping on a treed part of the path near the cliff's ledge. The sky was red, just as Dag had described, a magical display against the silhouettes of the pines. It was Sunday morning and Dag was now in his version of church. "Most people sleep through this," he said. "They don't even know what they miss."

By mid-morning we were back at Dag's camp. The late-autumn sun was now beaming through the trees, slowly thawing some of the snow and ice that surrounded our tents. Dag kicked out the embers of the fire and packed away his kettle, matches and anything else that might attract an animal. He put everything into a sealed bin. He gathered all but one of the books that had spilled out of his tent and zipped them back inside. Then he reached for his journal.

"I don't think a person with a journal can be lonely," he said. "I learned that from Nansen and Amundsen." He was referring to Fridtjof Nansen, a Norwegian polar explorer and the first person to successfully ski across Greenland, and another Norwegian, Roald Amundsen, the first person to successfully navigate the Northwest Passage. Dag explained: "When they felt lonely on their expeditions they would pull out their journals and write until they didn't feel lonely anymore. I do the same."

I asked if I could look at his journal. He brushed it off, then handed it to me and said: "There are no secrets in there."

I flipped it open. The first entry in the book noted that this was the 72nd in a series of journals. Dag started writing in this particular journal a week earlier, after he filled the previous one. He said the average journal lasted him about a month and although this one was labelled number 72, it was actually closer to number 500. He had been keeping a journal for more than 40 years.

"That's a lot of journals," I said. "Where do you keep them?"

"In my bus," he said.

I tried to visualize a bus with 500 journals inside. The one in my hand was a hardcover pocketbook about an inch thick, with 128 pages, many of them laminated with clear tape. On the cover was a child's pencil drawing of Dag on skis. It looked old, as if the drawing had been in his possession for decades before he taped it to the cover. On the spine were taped two sentences that Dag had cut out of a magazine: "Give peace a voice. Give solitude a place." On the back was a black-and-white photo of himself at the top of a mountain next to a young Nancy Greene. The photo was roughly 50 years old, from around the time of the 1968 Olympics in Grenoble, where Greene won gold in giant slalom. She looked as she did in most of the photos I had ever seen of her, but Dag looked very different. Young, dashing, kempt.

He said he tried to keep two journals on him at any given time, one for the present and one from the year earlier. Each day he recorded his time spent running. And each day he would go back to the previous year's entry in order to monitor his aging. It was his way of keeping tabs on his progress and decline. Though he wasn't tracking just his own progress and decline, but that of the world as well.

He started many days with a time-stamp: "*3 a.m., coffee purring.*" Then he recorded the weather: "*Starry night gives clear perspective on the size of one life.*" He followed that with the news of the hour: "*Paris is in lockdown, 120 dead. France mourns, vows revenge. The forever wars have no end. −10 last year on this morning. Big storm coming. Climate change. Got tons of food and eight litres of water. Should be snowing. Five hours run today. Getting up at 5 a.m. never fails. Everybody in A&W were sitting with their jackets. How little they understand their bodies. Maybe there's nothing to understand?"*

I was still reading when Dag explained a portion of what I was looking at: "Every day I look back one year to see what was happening and what I did on the same day. Then I know what I need to do to make today better. To improve on what I did before. The secret is don't lie to your journal. Otherwise it will never keep you honest."

His recorded thoughts were surrounded by clippings from news stories he taped to the page. The subjects varied but tended to deal with major social issues. One read: "There's an epidemic with 27 million victims. And no visible symptoms. Believe it or not, 27 million Americans are functionally illiterate." The cut-outs were often accompanied by anonymous quotes that he transcribed by hand—*"Success is just another opportunity to buy more stuff you don't need"*—and photos of anyone from Michael Caine to an elderly woman at a soup kitchen.

"Who are all these people?" I asked.

"People I once knew," he said.

I flipped through a few more pages before handing the journal back to him.

"People matter," he said.

The comment only made the mystery of his solitude more perplexing.

"It looks like you knew a lot of people," I said.

He took off his backpack and slipped the journal inside. "I never really knew my mother," he said. "I tried to find her once but she was already gone." He pulled his backpack over his shoulder and breathed in the cold air. For a moment he seemed to drift away to some other place.

I asked what he meant.

He came back to the present. "She died in a car accident," he said. "Somewhere in Sweden. I don't even know what she looked like."

It took a moment to reconcile what he had just said with the story he had previously shared about having been raised on a farm.

"What about your father?" I asked.

"He was a German soldier," Dag said. "I never knew his real name."

It was getting dark by the time Dag led us back down through the bone field and to the highway where our trek had started the day before. We climbed into Derek's car and made our way south through the Okanagan before veering east up another mountain as Dag directed us toward a dirt road that led toward the decaying school bus that was his home. The road was long and rough and filled with twists and turns. There was nothing in sight, no buildings or driveways, when Dag told us to stop. He said we were less than a kilometre from his home in the woods, but he insisted on travelling the rest of the way by foot. I shook his hand on the side of the road and told him that if he ever wanted help trying to find his parents, I would be willing to try to help him. I jotted my phone number on a piece of paper and tore it from my notebook. "Everyone deserves to know where they came from," I said.

He looked at the paper, then back at me. "It's not where you come from that matters so much as who you are," he said.

He tossed his bag over his shoulder and stepped off the road and into the bush. Myles, Derek and I got back into the car and watched as he disappeared into the forest. Then we headed to the airport.

FOUR

THE DEATH RACE

My humanity is a constant self-overcoming.
—FRIEDRICH NIETZSCHE, QUOTED
IN DAG'S JOURNALS

Nine months passed before I saw Dag again.

Back in Toronto I did what I always did. I moved on to the next story. I went to Everest, finished the book I was writing, then immersed myself in one magazine story after another. I spent time with wealthy entrepreneurs who had converted an old chocolate factory into the world's largest marijuana grow-op. And when I was done writing up their story I flew across the country to profile a former sniper and discuss the psychological toll of picking off Taliban fighters in Afghanistan. I travelled to Los Angeles and Vancouver to meet with retired football players who believed their brains were rotting inside their heads. Then I flew to Boston to interview scientists who were collecting the brains of deceased athletes, slicing them up and placing them under microscopes to study the impact of concussions. I was busy. But not a day went by that I didn't wonder about Dag.

I learned more about Dag in that first visit to his training camp than I learned from any of the stories written about him. He was an extreme athlete and a sage recluse, sure, but he was also a 74-year-old war orphan who believed his parents were a German soldier and a Norwegian woman.

There was a mystery about him that I wanted to solve. He would pop into my head at odd times. I had developed periodic sleeping issues that made me wake in the middle of the night, unable to get back to sleep. My preferred coping mechanism was usually to get out of bed and plough into work, even if it was three in the morning. Usually, after an hour or so, my brain would exhaust itself and I would be able to get back to sleep. Sometimes, however, I wouldn't make it back to bed. I would still be at the computer as the sky turned red over the city. In those moments, I would invariably think of Dag, running through the forest toward that lookout where the red sky filtered through the trees, and wonder whether he was still alive. Then I would find myself wandering down one online rabbit hole or another: Nazi genealogy, the past and present of extreme skiing, the health benefits (and detriments) of ultrarunning, the psychology of modern-day hermits. I was going deep on a lot of fronts, all in an effort to figure Dag out.

When I first set out to meet him I thought I was just going to write about a superhero for old people. Dag was a simple archetype in my mind, someone who was living by his own rules and pushing the boundaries of what seemed humanly possible in order to preserve his independence. But there was so much more to him than that.

By mid-summer 2016 I was back on a plane and heading out to see him again. This time, however, he was nowhere near his bus or his training camp. He was on the move, making his way to northern Alberta to compete in a torturous ultramarathon known as the Canadian Death Race—a 125-kilometre foot race that leads competitors up and down three mountains on the outskirts of Grande Cache and attracts only the fittest ultra-athletes.

IT WAS LATE on a hot July day when I connected with Dag for the second time. He had just finished hitchhiking his way into Grande Cache,

Alberta, a rugged mountain town on a high plateau, and recounted the three-day, 760-kilometre journey to me. He had made the trip 14 times over the past decade and a half, each time a little bit more battered than the last. This time he took a bus from the Okanagan Valley into the Monashee Mountains en route to Revelstoke and the golden corridor that leads caribou, wolves and tourists toward Jasper and the plains of northern Alberta.

He proceeded out of the town of Hinton, Alberta, on foot, breaking a trail through the tall grass and shallow gullies on the edge of the highway, choosing the path of most resistance instead of the paved shoulder. His eyes were squinted slits in the sun, but he kept them masked behind a pair of $5 shades he had purchased at a gas station five days earlier. His hair was long, knotted and wild and it bounced off his shoulders as he ran. He liked to run with nothing on other than a pair of black spandex shorts. His arms and legs were corded with muscles so visible on his fat-free frame that his every flex and release could be seen through his skin. Although his hair was white and the skin of his arms showed the common bruising of someone his age, he was fit. He could run for hours and walk for days with little rest and no nourishment beyond what he carried in the pack strapped over both shoulders.

He would have stood out to all who passed him on that mountain highway, not simply because he was the only human anyone would have seen on foot for miles, but because there was something fragile yet savagely fierce about his appearance. Only the tired look of his neon running shoes betrayed the reality that he had accumulated more mileage in those soles than was registered on some of the odometers of the transport trucks and camper vans that passed him every few minutes along the highway. He estimated that he had run more than 10,000 kilometres in those shoes alone—far enough that if he had run in a straight line they would have taken him all the way to Chile.

It was the older men in pickup trucks heading north who were the most likely to slow down as they passed and offer him a ride. But youthful couples on cross-country adventures stopped for him too. He didn't always climb inside. Sometimes he would look them over before carrying on. Other times he would just run on past, mindful not to slow his pace as he gained elevation, cresting one more mountain on his annual pilgrimage to the Death Race.

To most who transported him in their vans and pickup trucks, his name was as unusual as his appearance, let alone his mere presence on the highway. It was hard to imagine where he might fit in. He seemed even more out of place among other ultramarathoners, most of whom had made the long journey to Grande Cache over the Rockies or by rental car out of Edmonton International Airport.

It was 9 p.m., the late-night sun hovering on the horizon, when he wandered into town, dropped his backpack into a camper that belonged to a Grande Cache resident and headed out in search of food. Grande Cache was bustling, having attracted athletes and superathletes from across the country and a few from other parts of the world. All through town, competitors checked into hotels and were now measuring their caloric intakes, consuming light, digestible foods like energy bars and electrolyte beverages, or lying on their beds, stretching their ankles and resting their knees for what lay ahead. But not the old man. He sat alone in a pizza parlour, eating lasagna and drinking lager.

It was pushing 11 and just after twilight when he returned to the camper, fired up a stove and began heating water. He opened his pack, pulled out a couple of the potatoes he had carried into town on his back and dropped them in the pot to boil. Then he climbed under a sleeping bag, pulled out his journal and began to write.

"Thunderstorm warning for tomorrow. Stabbing in France—19 people killed in Japan—the disease is spreading."

It was nearly midnight by the time he fell asleep.

FOR 15 YEARS, Dag had been coming to the Death Race to push his body further and faster than many of his fellow competitors, the majority of them less than half his age. He had completed the race a record seven times, each time as its oldest competitor. But now seven long years had passed since he last crossed the finish line. And though he was markedly slower at 75 than he had been at 69, he refused to give up. When he ran, he did so for sport, for pleasure and for his own survival.

But there was something fleeting to it all—a general understanding that if he ever stopped running, he would stop existing altogether. As one of his fellow contestants noted, Dag seemed to have "an ephemeral, monk-like presence" on the trail. His slow yet relentless style appeared almost spiritual and evoked comparisons to the legendary Japanese monks of Mount Hiei who run-walk 1,000 marathons in 1,000 days in order to attain enlightenment. But he also evoked comparisons to a freak of nature: a veritable Wolverine who, like the tortured mutant from the X-Men comic books, seemed to age slower than anyone else and had a capacity to withstand inhuman degrees of pain and keep pushing forward.

At any given time he looked the part of both a battle-hardened warrior and a sage old mystic. It was the latter image that tended to endear him to most people—especially when he slowed his pace approaching a fellow runner who was keeled over in pain and on the brink of collapse. He would appear to them like some half-naked septuagenarian messiah, his figure distorted through their sweat-blurred vision as he planted his feet next to theirs, placed his hand on their shoulder and imparted some ancient-sounding wisdom.

One racer would later recall Dag's words like so: "Look down. It does not matter where your feet were yesterday, or where they are going to be tomorrow. It matters where your feet are at this moment."

THE SUN HAD not yet risen over the hills when Dag opened his eyes. He checked his watch. It was 5:43—an early start to what would be one of the most gruelling days of his life. While he boiled water for his instant coffee, he opened his journal and began to write. "*Feel good on this important morning. No boring days.*" He looked out the window of the camper and up at the sky. Then back to his journal. "*Overcast. X my fingers it won't rain.*"

He sipped his coffee until it was gone. Then he placed the boiled potatoes into his pack, put on his running shorts and tied his running shoes and made his way toward the start line where the other Death Racers were quickly gathering. He navigated his way through a crowd of men and women with Kinesio tape all over their legs. He never liked to start a race from anywhere but the very back of the herd. It allowed him to slip into his own meditative rhythm. He stood back from the start line and breathed in the optimism of the first-time competitors while filtering out the sound of the beats pumping out of the loudspeakers nearby. He preferred to listen to the beat of his own heart when he ran. It was the inner metronome he kept pace to. Two beats to every step; three, if he was going uphill. There was a synchronization between heart and mind when he really got moving, when he swore he could feel his pulse inside his own brain. That's when the endorphins would kick in, creating a runner's high that he called his "gateway to clarity." Once he passed through that gateway, he could hold his pace for several hours.

The clock ticked down toward 8 a.m., and soon a rush of the youngest, most competitive runners pushed over the start line, beginning a race that would take roughly 24 hours for most to complete. None knew what lay before them, that by nightfall some runners in a hypothermic state would be rescued while others would be treated for exhaustion.

Dag watched the first few hundred racers disappear into the forest, heading along a mud-soaked trail that would lead them 19 kilometres toward an abandoned rail line and onward to the base of an 1,800-metre mountain.

The herd was thinning out, the race already several minutes old when he finally pressed his finger to his stopwatch and began to move. He was all alone as he crossed the start line, an elderly man who had already fallen behind the pack. He was last, but he was just getting started.

Dag knew his body couldn't move like it used to but he was determined to push it as hard as he could for as long as possible. It didn't bother him that he was losing momentum. He knew that ultimately his days as a Death Racer would end, not because he couldn't handle the race, but because his body would slow to such a pace that he would fail to reach the first checkpoint before the cut-off time. The prospect that someday he would be told that he was essentially too old and too slow to even start the race didn't bother him either. Because that day still seemed distant.

Dag competing in the 125-kilometre Canadian Death Race at the age of 75. (Courtesy of Derek Frankowski)

It was curiosity and desire, not ego, that drove Dag back to the Death Race again and again. Despite his advancing years, his best finish had not been his first, but rather his third, when, at the age of 64, he crossed the finish line after 20 hours and 56 minutes—one minute and 54 seconds faster than he had run at the age of 62. What he craved above all was the magical feeling he experienced most often on the trails near his bus when he would reach a marker in the bush and check his stopwatch, only to surprise himself that he was running faster than he had run in several years. He lived for those moments, rare as they were now, because it was then that he felt a connection to something preternatural. "It's like touching the fountain of youth," Dag had told me. "Juan Ponce de León went looking in the wrong place. He didn't need to sail to Florida. All he needed was a stopwatch, a journal and a pair of running shoes."

EIGHT HOURS LATER, the sun was high, yet lost behind a thickening wall of cloud that cast a cold, dull shadow over the entire Sulphur River valley. All that any of the 203 trail runners working their way through that valley could see when they looked into the sky were warnings of the storm rolling in from the north. There was nothing any of them could do to avoid nature's intent. So they pushed and dragged their bodies around the 125-kilometre mud-sloped inclines and exhausting switchbacks that made up the Death Race.

There were inherent risks associated with running such a long distance, but no one went into the Death Race expecting to die. And yet like any ultramarathon, the race had a way of making you feel like you were pushing toward death. Much of that came from the reality that running such distances demanded much more than the expected wear on the joints, muscles and ligaments. It disrupted multiple parts of the body's internal function, the most common being the diversion of blood from the racers' stomachs and into their muscles, stopping their digestion and causing uncontrolled nausea. Sometimes a racer would double over with stomach pain or turn their head sideways and vomit over their shoulder while they ran. Some experienced temporary loss of vision as their corneas swelled from a buildup of fluid. Then there were those who would end up so fatigued on the trail that they would begin to hallucinate. They were the ones who could prove a danger to themselves, seeing and hearing things along the trail that weren't really there and, in the most problematic cases, wandering into the wilderness and getting lost. However, none of that was as concerning as the weather.

The air had been cooling for hours as an Arctic front rolled in from the north. It was nearly 4 p.m., and though there were technically still six hours of daylight, a dark shroud had set in. The winds howled over the mountains as the barometric pressure began to plunge. One hundred runners had already abandoned the race, and those who were still competing were now spread out over 40 kilometres of trail. Most of them were low, near the valley floor. But a lone man could still be seen chugging his way upwards, navigating a narrow ridge lined with edelweiss, boulders and shale. He ran like an old tractor, durable but slow and pushing the boundary of obsolescence. He had been running at his full capacity for nearly eight hours, working his way up the same mountain for the better part of the afternoon. He gained more than a kilometre of elevation along the way. He could feel the temperature changing against his skin, which was beginning to shiver in the cold. And he could feel it in his joints, which were beginning to ache as the already inflamed tissue in his knees, hips, ankles and fingers began to expand, sending twinges of pain through his body. He was sore, though he did not allow it. Tired, though he did not know it. And he was hungry, though he did not show it, not as he propelled himself above the tree line and toward Grande Mountain's rough-cut peak. He was more than 40 kilometres into the race but he was showing his age on the trail. It had been seven years since he successfully finished a Death Race, and though he had been training nearly every day since, the intervening years had taken their toll and slowed his pace. He could still run the distance, but he was a decade older than anyone else in the race and running up against the cut-off times at every checkpoint.

Derek Frankowski and I had been monitoring Dag's progress from the sidelines, navigating our way to the checkpoints ourselves, either on foot or by car. We hitched a ride up Grande Mountain in the back of a Suzuki Sidekick that never got out of first gear. The wind howled through the valley below as we stepped out of the truck and made our way to the checkpoint at the peak of Grande Mountain. We watched as Dag crossed with a few minutes to spare and took in the view without slowing his pace. He could see the periodic explosion of lightning over the mountains on the horizon. Then came the thunder. He counted the distance in his head. The rain was still a few kilometres away, but he knew that once it hit, the trail beneath his feet would become unpredictable and treacherous. Unable to quicken his pace, he continued down the other side of the mountain.

His steps were wobbly as he began his descent, striking a precarious balance between speed and control as he pushed himself downward. The downhills were tough on the knees, spines and ankles of all competitors, especially the older ones, whose joints contained less lubricating fluid and had thinner layers of cartilage due to years of wear and tear—part of the many ways the human body disintegrates over time. Most elite runners reach their peak between ages 30 and 35. Then muscle mass, bone density and maximal aerobic capacity begin to decrease. And though some runners do manage to run faster at age 50 than they did at 35, it is generally because they performed below their capacity when they were younger. Athletes running at their peak will experience a gradual trail-off from age 35, and by 50 they will have lost roughly two minutes and 45 seconds per year over the course of a 42.2-kilometre marathon. After age 60, the performance declines become more drastic as the human stride shortens and ankle power decreases.

For all Dag knew, his capacity as an ultramarathon runner had probably peaked in the early 1970s, when he was in his early 30s. But he had only just begun running at that time and had confined himself to simple marathons while also living the life of a professional skier in winter and working as a full-time logger during the summers. He ran his first marathon in northern Washington in his early 30s—in a pair of jeans and without training. He finished in just under four hours, which put him in the range of intermediate runners in his age group. He competed in 10 more marathons before he was 50. In his late 40s, his finishing times were hovering around 3 hours and 20 minutes. He was fast enough to qualify for the Boston Marathon but he never bothered to enter. By his late 50s he had also taken up competitive cross-country skiing, and by the time he turned 61 he was a Canadian championship ski racer, placing fourth in his age group at the 2002 Masters World Cup cross-country ski race in Quebec despite never having had a coach. Then someone slapped a promotional flyer for the Death Race onto a table while he was eating and said, "Here's something you're probably too old to do."

Dag was 62 when he hitched a ride to Grande Cache and entered his first Death Race. He finished in a gruelling 20 hours, 58 minutes and 16 seconds. The next year he crossed the finish line in 23 hours and 48 seconds. Then he came back again 12 months later, at the age of 64, and posted his personal best—20 hours and 56 minutes. He ran an average of six kilometres an hour during that year's race, covering roughly 560 metres more each hour than he had the year before. He used that personal best as the benchmark to track his aging and his decline up until 2009, when he finished the race for the last time in 23 hours, 5 minutes and 26 seconds, his pace having dropped back to roughly the same as it was when he was five years younger. It was the last time he was able to complete the entire 125-kilometre circuit in the requisite 24 hours.

But he never stopped trying, and every subsequent year that he fell short of the 125-kilometre mark, he succeeded in finishing what race organizers called the Near Death Marathon, a 49-kilometre ultra that was itself 7.8 kilometres longer than a regulation marathon. The Near Death Marathon, which was essentially the first half of the Death Race, had its own designated cut-off time—9.5 hours—meant to safeguard both the competitive nature of the contest and the health of its contestants. In 2010 Dag had completed the Near Death Marathon with 45 minutes to spare and used that feat as the new barometer by which to challenge his body as he entered his 70s. In 2011 he actually got faster, shedding 28 minutes from his previous year's time.

Though Dag was always the oldest person on the trail, he was inspired by runners even older than him who continued to compete in more traditional marathons around the world. Among them was the Sikh road runner Fauja Singh, who in 2011, at the age of 100, became the first centenarian to complete an organized marathon when he finished the Toronto Waterfront Marathon. Dag had read about Singh in the *Globe and Mail*, cut out the article and taped it into one of his journals for inspiration. Singh was born in British India in 1911 and was so malnourished as a boy that he did not walk until the age of five. He lived through partition and the birth of modern India and was already beyond his life expectancy when, in the mid-1990s, he took up running as a means of therapy after the deaths of his wife, a son and a daughter. He competed in his first organized marathon at 89 and set his personal best aged 92, when he completed the Flora London Marathon in 6 hours and 54 minutes.

Singh, who credited his physical longevity to abstaining from smoking and alcohol and to a vegetarian diet, lived on the outskirts of London, England, trained primarily on asphalt and subsisted on a simple diet of phulka, dal, green vegetables, yogurt and milk. Compared to Dag, Singh treated his body like a temple. "I take lots of water and tea with ginger," he told a reporter with the *Indian Express* in 2004. "I go to bed early taking the name of my *Rabba* [God] as I don't want all those negative thoughts crossing my mind." Like Dag, Singh started every day with a long-distance run and, like Dag, the act itself was almost spiritual. "The first 20 miles are not difficult," Singh said of his experiences as a marathon runner. "As for the last six miles, I run while talking to God."

Dag didn't speak to God as he ran, but he did speak of a more personal transcendence, which he struggled to describe, other than to say that it was when he was nearing exhaustion that he felt closest to his own mortality. "I have to push to my limitations in order to accept my limitations," he said.

He viewed age as a "state of mind" rather than an actual figure. He had read articles—which he also cut out and taped into his journals—about scientific studies that found age-related deterioration to be the side effect of a sedentary lifestyle rather than of aging. He lived by the belief that he could modulate his decline through increased training. And so he ran like few others on the planet and nobody else his age. He had worn through an average of two and a half pairs of running shoes each year ever since 1978, when he started recording such things. It's how he knew that the Hokas on his feet were the 85th pair he had bought in a long line of shoes that he used to clock hundreds of thousands of kilometres over the course of the previous 40 years.

Though he accepted that he was moving slower, Dag tried to maintain the total distance he ran each year by simply increasing the hours he spent training. Where once he could routinely run 10 kilometres in under 40 minutes, it now took him over an hour. He once read that the average human walks roughly 2,200 kilometres a year, a pace that would take them roughly 18 years to circumnavigate the globe. By contrast, Dag ran about 8,000 kilometres a year. He had reflected on that math, drawn up some calculations, and realized that despite his age he was running the equivalent of the entire equator once every five years. He had the logbooks to prove it.

Incredibly, by my calculations, he may have run enough miles during his lifetime to cover the distance between Earth and the moon. Dag shook his head in bewilderment when I told him how far I believed he had travelled. Then he smiled and paraphrased a quote from his childhood hero, Fridtjof Nansen, the Norwegian explorer who led the first crossing of Greenland on skis: "If it's difficult, I'll do it right away. If it's impossible, it will take a little longer."

TIME STALKS EVERYONE, but when it catches up with a professional athlete, it can be brutal to watch. It's why so many of the greatest names in sport often fade from the spotlight once they leave the field, to age out of sight. And it's why, at 5:25 p.m. on July 31, 2016, Derek, myself and others stood at the 49-kilometre checkpoint of the Death Race willing the oldest contestant in the race to materialize before the 9.5-hour cut-off. He was well out of sight, having just run through a cemetery as storm clouds thickened overhead. The skin on his bare legs contracted against the cold as he propelled himself through the cemetery and back into town. His shoes were wearing out, his toes bleeding through his wool socks. He could feel the dampness of his blood cooling against his feet as he planted each step into the gravel on the only route back into Grande Cache.

Derek and I waited near the centre of town, next to a nursing station where a middle-aged racer shivered under a thermal blanket. More and more competitors were now abandoning the race as the temperature dropped toward zero. A race steward's radio crackled at the nursing station. "We've got heavy winds at the top of Hamell," the voice said. Mount Hamell was the next major peak in Dag's path—a 2,100-metre mountain, the highest summit on the Death Race—a stunning strata with a swooping lookout that offered no protection from the elements. The route near the top of the mountain was devoid of much vegetation longer than grass. Then another voice came over the radio. It said that organizers were preparing to retrieve runners breaking down on the mountainside.

A crash of thunder echoed through the valley. A steward looked at the race clock and then at the open road. It was 5:26 p.m.—9 hours and 26 minutes since the start of the race. A skeletal figure could be seen cresting the horizon. His pace was steady but slow—the same as it had been seven hours earlier when I watched him run along an abandoned railway track. His feet chugged along the pavement, and he was humming again—"As Time Goes By."

The race clock registered 9:29:31 when Dag crossed the 49-kilometre checkpoint. He had reached the cut-off with 29 seconds to spare. Someone offered him water. He took a sip, handed back the paper cup, stood with his hands on his waist and looked at the storm over Hamell. It was another 21 kilometres to reach the next checkpoint. I knew, and he knew, as did the stewards watching him, that if he carried on with the race he was destined to get disqualified at the next cut-off. He looked back to the nursing station.

"I guess this is far enough for one day," he said.

He raised his arms, filled his lungs with the cold air, looked at his time on the race clock and shook his head. It was the worst time he had ever recorded.

"Look at that," he said. "A new record to break."

FIVE

ON AGING

Self-preservation is the antidote for panic.
—DAG'S JOURNALS

Dag paced inside a dark and musty trailer, listening to the thunder and the rain ricocheting off the thin metal roof over his head. The trailer belonged to a Grande Cache local who allowed him to sleep in it while he was in town for the race. Dag had consumed a six-pack of warm Kokanee beer and now he watched as lightning illuminated his reflection in the window. Derek and I had watched him abuse his body on the trail and now we were sitting with him as he drank himself to sleep. Six hours had passed since he had dropped out of the Death

Race for what would be the last time. Another 120 runners had suffered the same fate—several were rescued from the slopes of Mount Hamell where the temperature had plunged below freezing and the rain turned to snow. There were still 84 runners out there, weathering the storm, periodically screaming into the sleet as they ran, trying to find whatever it was they needed to push through it.

Part of Dag wished he was still out there with them. He had travelled to Grande Cache with a vision of doing what no one thought possible—completing the full 125-kilometre Death Race at the age of 75. He had trained to go the distance and he still had energy to burn. But the conditions were dangerous, and now he was getting drunk.

It was just before midnight when Derek and I left the trailer and ran back to our motel through the rain. Dag fell asleep shortly after our departure. It was still dark when he awoke, though the rain had stopped. He slept with his shoes on, and when he rose from his bed he quickly climbed out the trailer door and made for the finish line. The race was entering its 20th hour, and he wanted to be at the finish when the competitors started to make their way in. There was a racer there when he arrived, covered in mud and clutching his chest for warmth as attendants gathered around, draping a blanket over his shoulders. Dag watched as another runner approached the finish, wincing as he crossed. They were coming in now at a rate of one every 10 minutes—many of them looking defeated, even in their victory. Dag watched as the families and friends of the racers wrapped them in warm embraces. He stood alone and away from the gathering, and then he turned and started to run through the town's streets. His legs were stiff, his feet raw. He felt sluggish, but he continued to push forward, his body struggling to clear itself of the previous night's alcohol. He didn't allow himself to focus on the pain and kept his mind on his surroundings instead. The sun was making its way over the mountains to the east. Day was breaking, and Dag was on the move once more.

By nine he had collected his backpack and was ready for the long journey home. I found him sitting alone on a couch inside a coffee shop, chronicling the previous day's experience in his journal.

"*Can't buy a run in the Death Race, it has to be experienced,*" he wrote. "*It shows you your place in society.*" Then he wrote a sentence that seemed to resonate with him: "*Mediocrity consumes quality.*"

He was doubling back over those letters with

his pen, making them stand out on the page, when I sat down beside him, said good morning and asked how he was feeling.

An ultramarathon's after-effects on the human body can be summed up in a single word: traumatic. A runner can lose almost half an inch in height as their back muscles tense up while much-needed fluid is diverted away from the intervertebral discs. It can take days for the fluid levels to be replaced, delaying a runner's return to size. The sheer duration of the exertion involved can cause physiological damage to multiple organs including the heart, liver and kidneys. The damage is usually temporary. The prolonged deprivation of basic nutrients causes its own problems, as does the undulating nature of the trail, which can wreak havoc on a runner's muscles. Significant damage is often inflicted during the downhills, when the muscles contract while elongated under the load of every step, creating a wobbly sensation that can cause runners to slow their descent as they work against gravity. The slowing movements cause muscle fibres to tear by the millions at the molecular level, leaving markers of cellular damage to accumulate in the blood. It's partly why health professionals recommend that anyone who has put their body through the devastation of such an event allow weeks to recover.

Dag coughed as he said good morning. He cleared his throat, caught his breath and insisted that he felt fantastic. "My knees were a bit stiff when I woke up," he said, "so I went out for a morning run." His response was entirely in character, but still hard to believe. He had run for nearly nine and a half hours the day before, absorbing the shock of more than 75,000 steps, then drunk himself to sleep, only to rise before dawn and head out once again.

I offered to drive him part of the way home. We left Grande Cache and headed for the open road, snaking south toward Jasper. There seemed a finality to the journey; a realization, at least by me, that he might never get back to this place to compete in another Death Race. It seemed doubtful that he could race again when he was already brushing up to within seconds of the race's long-established cut-offs.

I asked if it made him sad knowing that he was essentially too old for the race. He raised his twisted fingers in front of his chin, as if grabbing at a concept he had been moulding with his arthritic hands.

"You can't dwell on what has been lost," he said. "Life survives by carrying on. You never see an animal stand at a crossroads for long."

Then he lowered his hands and reached into

the backpack he kept squared between his feet in the car. He pulled out the weekend edition of the *Globe and Mail*, then took a pen from the pencil case that doubled as his wallet. On the newspaper's front page he drew what looked like the side cut of a descending staircase. "This is the way I try to live," he said. Each of the steps was a plateau that represented a period of time in his natural decline. "The peak is behind me, but the plateaus are ahead. Any time spent on a plateau is a gift, especially at my age." He pressed the pen onto one of the plateaus he had drawn and wrote the numbers *9:29:31*. "This is where I am now. Maybe I'm at the start of the plateau, maybe I'm at the other end of it."

"Is there no point where you think you might retire from all this?" I asked. "You know, like, take it easy?"

"Take it easy?" he replied. "Every day, we get to make a choice between trying to do something for what might be the last time or not trying at all. That's what it is to age. I might never be able to do again what I did yesterday, but I'm going to keep trying," he said. "I'd rather live like that than on a couch with a remote in my hand."

Then he said something that stuck with me.

"Time matters most when time is running out."

The sky was grey as we rolled down the Yellowhead Highway. Dag pressed his hand to the glass. Then he opened the window. A rush of air flowed through the rented Chevy. He breathed it in and poked his head out toward the chiselled mountains closing in on the highway as we made our way closer to Jasper. There was a chill to the air. He closed his eyes and let the wind blast against his face. Then he closed the window and looked forward.

"Do you want to know the secret of longevity?" he asked.

"Definitely," I replied.

"Don't fill your life with things to worry about. If you start to worry about one thing, you worry about everything. The weather, money, other people, your car, your house, the grass."

"Do you think your children worry about you?" I asked.

We hadn't spoken much about his children in our previous encounter. I knew he had three from his marriage, but I wasn't sure whether he had more. I was under the impression that only one of his children was willing to speak with him. The others hadn't been in contact for years. I didn't know what had caused the fallout, but I wondered if it was the inevitable consequence of having an elderly father who lived in the wild and only checked in periodically when he ran into town and located a payphone. His youngest daughter was the only one he kept in touch with. She never knew when he would call her, and when he did, it was generally from a random or unknown number. She had steeled her mind a long time ago to the possibility that one day he would stop calling altogether, or worse, that she would answer a call from a stranger only to learn that a hiker had stumbled over Dag's remains in a forest somewhere.

It wasn't clear whether Dag understood the toll his way of life took on his children. But it was clear that he was unwilling—or unable—to change for any of them. His freedom was paramount to his sense of self, and he could think of no reason why anyone should object to the way he lived his life. In Dag's mind he was neither poor nor homeless. He had $1,540 in the bank and survived on Canada's Old Age Security program and the Canada Pension Plan, receiving $1,700 a month, or $20,400 a year. He spent most of that money on food, beer and reading material, and though he managed to keep a positive balance in his bank account, he couldn't afford a change in lifestyle even if he wanted one.

"The most dangerous place in the world is the comfort zone," he told me. "It kills people. I don't see why anyone would worry about me.

Some people see me and they think, 'That guy needs help.' But I don't need any help. I am independent. Not everyone sees that, because they see my clothes or my hair or the stick I carry over my shoulder and they can't understand why I'm smiling. Well, I'm smiling because I'm happy. And I'm happy because I'm living my life the way I want to live it."

Then he told me the story of his adoptive father. How he had always seemed young up to the day that he turned 50. "Then everyone told him he was old," Dag said. "And he made the mistake of believing them." Dag pointed to his own heart. "So he became old, on the inside. Our society treats old people the same as children. We talk down to the elderly. It's as if society says you reach a certain age and you're not important anymore."

He went quiet, and both of us stared out at the open road. I brought the conversation back to his children. "You have three kids?" I asked.

He kept looking out the window as he listed off their individual successes. The eldest was married, had children of her own and was living on a farm in Saskatchewan. Though he did not say so, he hadn't seen her in 20 years and hadn't met her children either. Dag knew he was a grandfather, but didn't know his grandchildren's names. His two youngest kids were twins—a boy and a girl. His son's name was Hans. Hans was married and living in the southern Okanagan. Dag had mentioned Hans many times before, but he never let on that they hadn't seen each other in a decade.

Then Dag shared something unexpected with me. He had another child. Another boy whose name Dag didn't know. The child had been the result of a short-lived relationship with a Chilean woman he met while working as a ski instructor in Santiago. He said he thought of both of them often, but he had no idea how to reach out to either of them. He didn't think it would be a good idea anyway. Fifty years had passed since the child was born, and as far as he knew, the boy didn't even know that Dag was his father. Dag was living alone at Whistler when he received an envelope in the mail all the way from Chile. Inside was a black-and-white photo of a child. There was no return address on the accompanying letter. Two words were written on the back of the photo: "*Tu hijo*," it read, in Spanish. Your son.

IT WAS EARLY afternoon when we finally rolled into Jasper, passing wild Stone sheep, elk and a lone grey wolf in the middle of the highway on our way into town. I slowed for the wolf and watched as it neither quickened its pace, altered its course nor acknowledged our presence as we approached.

"It's as if he doesn't know we're here," I said.

"He knows," Dag replied. We watched as the wolf carried on slowly toward the shoulder and into the brush. Then we carried on. I parked the car, and as we climbed out I noticed Dag's arm was covered with dried blood. His skin was paper-thin and bruised and looked as though he had snagged it on something during the race.

"You're hurt," I said.

He rolled his arm from side to side and looked at the blood. It was all over his elbow and his arm and appeared to have come from his bicep.

"The parts are old," he said. "But the machine still works. It will heal."

SIX

THE STORIES WE DON'T TELL

The more identities a man has, the more they express the person they conceal.
—JOHN LE CARRÉ, *TINKER, TAILOR, SOLDIER, SPY*

I sat awake, staring out into the dark sky on the red-eye flight back to Toronto after another three days spent in Dag's orbit. I had driven him as far as Jasper. We said goodbye next to a railroad track, then I doubled back to catch a plane out of Edmonton. I wondered, as I left him, whether I would ever see him again. I was starting to view Dag as the most anomalous person I had ever met. I had convinced myself earlier that I understood the physical demands of his way of life, but the full emotional and mental complexity of his situation had escaped me. He was an old man who abused his body as if it were eternal. And he was what many would consider a homeless man who chose to live in the forest. And he was an orphan who didn't know where he had come from. And he was a father who didn't know all of his children.

He was no longer just the subject of a story on my desk. He was beginning to tie into my own understanding of how the pain and hurt of one generation gets passed down to the next.

When I set out to write about him, I didn't intend to become part of the story. But the more time I spent with him, the more I realized that the journalistic interest I had in solving the mysteries at the core of Dag's life were being driven by my own failures to solve some of the mysteries at the centre of mine.

Shortly before joining Dag at the Death Race, I had embarked on a 2,000-kilometre road trip from Dallas to Toronto with my 70-year-old father. We drove north along Route 66, cutting our way through Oklahoma, Missouri and Illinois before rolling into Chicago, the city of my grandmother's youth. We found our way to my grandmother's childhood home and reconnected with our family's roots before carrying on to the US-Canada border. On the last day of our travels we drove through Brantford, Ontario, where my father's father was born and where he had been resting under a pine tree since November 1967. My grandfather was an abusive alcoholic who alienated himself from his entire family, including my grandmother, who left him in 1966 after 32 years of marriage. He died of a heart attack in the passenger seat of a Mercury in a hospital parking lot, leaving my grandmother, my father and my aunt with years of psychological baggage to unpack. My grandfather had been born after his father died of tuberculosis in a Buffalo, New York, hospital just a few months earlier. As the only heir to a family estate, he inherited a large sum of money when he turned 19. But he subsequently lost the majority of that wealth in the stock market through the Great Depression, and by the middle of the 1930s he had relocated to India, along with my grandmother, to work as an engineer in Calcutta. By the time the Second World War began, very little was left of the money he had inherited, and when he returned from combat in Germany he was filled with rage. He spent the next two decades living with a wife and children who learned to fear him. My grandfather never took the time to get to know his son (my father) before he dropped dead in that parking lot. I was born 16 years after he died, but I understood from an early age that my own childhood was shaped by the scars of my father's upbringing and the unresolved issues he carried with him through his life.

Near the end of my grandmother's life she informed my father that despite everything he thought he knew about himself, he hadn't actually been his parents' first-born child. She told him that he had two other siblings but they had died in India. She told him their names but he was too shocked to ask any questions about their lives and the circumstances of their deaths. My father and his mother avoided further discussion about the children, and when my grandmother died any chance for clarity died with her. I later wondered what impact those children's deaths had had on my father's dysfunctional upbringing and how that upbringing had affected mine. The search for answers led me to Calcutta to wander through Christian cemeteries searching for my uncles' graves. I never found anything.

All of this had shaped my view of the world as a journalist and as a person. Often, when I interviewed someone, I ended up asking them about their childhood and about the things they had inherited from those who had come before. I wasn't always conscious of why this line of questioning fascinated me, but it left me with a collection of published stories about people with complex upbringings that had shaped their lives. Although I didn't yet understand how or why, I was self-aware enough to know that the inherent complexities in my relationship with my father and my father's father contributed to my desire to help Dag in his own quest to trace his origins.

It was nearly two years before I saw Dag again after saying goodbye in Jasper. Two years of periodically wondering if he was still out there, running through the wild, day and night. Every few months, consumed by curiosity, I would call the sports pub where his picture hung next to the door and ask if anyone had seen him. Weeks would pass and then my phone would ring and display "No Caller ID." Sometimes I was in a checkout line, other times in a classroom full of journalism students. More often than not, I missed the call. Dag always left a message on my phone. The messages often told a similar story. He started his voicemails explaining how he had run into town a few weeks earlier and been given my message at the pub. Then he had disappeared into the forest for a few weeks, only to call me back the next time he found himself near a payphone.

In the spring of 2018 he was 77 years old and reeling from a series of injuries when we connected on the phone. On that call we ended up talking about what he knew and what he didn't about where he had come from and why. I offered once more to try to help him find information about his biological parents. "You really believe there's anything to be found?" he asked me. I told him I didn't know, but that if he really wanted to know where he had come from, I was willing to help. He appreciated the offer and gave me carte blanche to get in contact with any family or friends if I thought it would help to find out anything about his parentage. "I don't believe you'll find anything," he told me. "The files you're looking for were probably taken back to Berlin and burned a long time ago."

And so I began sending out letters and emails to Dag's long-lost friends and family, as well as to officials on the other side of the world, enquiring about a boy who had one day materialized under mysterious circumstances on a Norwegian farm in the middle of a war. It would be a long time before I managed to piece together the earliest parts of his life. Even longer before I understood how these had shaped him into the old man I came to know.

For months after his arrival at the farm, the child who would become known as Dag didn't say a word. Not to the man and woman who carried him home from the capital, nor to the woodsmen who lived in the trapper cabins on the couple's lands, working the forests that rolled west from the river valley and stretched into the hills beyond the white wood manor that would become the boy's home from the moment his adoptive mother and father carried him inside until the day, six years later, when they would lift him from his bedroom floor and carry him away to the far side of the world for his own safety. No, the newly rechristened boy did not speak to anyone.

His new parents couldn't understand why he refused to speak. He was still a toddler, but he had been talkative when they met him in the orphanage next to the prison in the heart of Nazi-occupied Oslo. His earliest words, however, were lost to the world he left behind. He had spent the first year of his life with his birth mother in an Oslo hotel. The hotel stretched an entire city block and was situated in what had become a vibrant, central neighbourhood of the German regime. There were eight Norwegians for every Nazi in Norway, but the signs of German rule were everywhere. Barricades stopped the free flow of civilians through the streets, U-boats floated in the harbours next to battle cruisers and troop transports, while the Gestapo knocked on doors in the night, dragging out enemies of the Reichskommissariat Norwegen—the German civilian regime—to be questioned and tortured. Meanwhile, in the former residence of the Norwegian crown prince, the ruthless German tyrant Josef Terboven lived in opulence. As leader of the German administration in Norway, Terboven oversaw everything from massacres to concentration camps to the administration of Vidkun Quisling's ineffectual puppet government.

Terboven's rule was punctuated by the disappearance of Norwegian men in the night. Some would re-emerge, unable or unwilling to speak of what had happened to them. Others were never seen again. That was Oslo in the first years of Dag's life.

Fear reigned supreme in the capital, but the Nazis' hold on the country was far from absolute. An organized resistance movement had taken shape shortly after the invasion. First it was just teachers and schoolchildren wearing paper clips on their lapels to signify allegiance to their exiled king. Then it was women fashioning patriotic jewellery out of Norwegian coins. Hidden from sight, however, were the armed partisans who organized into what became known as the Norwegian Hjemmefronten (Home Front).

Armed and trained by British intelligence officers, the Hjemmefronten were saboteurs and commandos whose successes were countered by a series of German reprisals that left parts of Norway devastated. When members of the

Hjemmefronten ambushed two German police officers in a village in central Norway, Terboven responded by imposing martial law and ordering the execution of 10 prominent residents as "atonement sacrifices." That was in October 1942. Six months earlier, the Germans had razed an entire seaside village after discovering that the village had helped British-trained commandos who infiltrated Norway aboard fishing boats. The reprisals left the Norwegian people divided. On one side were the collaborationists who had chosen to join the German cause. On the other side were those who vowed to fight the Nazis by any means necessary.

For all their military strength and authority, the Germans in Norway remained vulnerable, as the number of Norwegian patriots far outnumbered the Nazi collaborationists. The size and reach of the Resistance was a constant problem for the Germans, but it was also a cause for trepidation among the collaborationists, especially those who could not easily defend themselves. Few were more vulnerable than the mothers of children born to German soldiers. Life on the streets of Oslo could be dangerous for women who were believed to have slept with the enemy.

It was partly for this reason that the Germans imported into Norway the program known as the Lebensborn. The chosen mothers experienced a life inside those commandeered hotels that was far less stark than it was in the rest of Oslo, where civilians were slowly starving. Resentment quickly grew among the general population, which had been forced to subsist on rations of nearly half their pre-war caloric intake. The women who bore the children of Nazi soldiers were among the most despised and vilified by the Norwegian patriots. They were viewed as opportunists and traitors and denounced with a label that stuck for years: *tyskertøser*—"Nazi whores."

This was the world into which the boy who would become Dag Aabye appeared to have been born. For the first seven months of his life he lived in a hotel with his mother. Then, shortly before Christmas 1941, she deposited him into a state-run orphanage and walked away. He spent the next 10 months of his life in the secure facility next to Oslo's main prison, where Norwegian patriots were trucked into holding cells to be beaten and forgotten. Life inside the Åkeberg children's home was as normal as could be for the earliest-born orphans of the war. Every day had the same rhythm, and the children inside were too young to understand the fullness of the horror going on in the Nazi-occupied streets beyond the orphanage walls.

One day in July 1942, Dag's 32-year-old

mother entered the justice department of the Reichskommissariat to sign away the rights to her 14-month-old child. Dag was too young to remember the name his birth mother gave him. Before long, he forgot her face, too. Over the next few months, those running the orphanage looked for parents best suited to keep him safe through to the end of the war and beyond.

Days turned to weeks inside the children's home, weeks to months, and soon all the boy knew was the crib that had become his home in the high-ceilinged ward filled with other children in other cribs. Life inside the home was loud, yet orderly. Children arrived and children departed by design. Only the least fortunate ever stayed long enough to fully understand where they were or why.

Then one day, a man and a woman arrived from the countryside. They took one look at the blond little boy and fell in love with him.

It was Wednesday, September 9, 1942, when for the very first time Helga Aabye held the child who would become her only son. She already knew the name she wanted to give him once they got him home. It would be another seven weeks before she and her husband, Georg, were granted approval to pack him up and take him with them to live on their farm. It was hard to refuse the couple's credentials. The 33-year-old Helga and

39-year-old Georg were wealthy landowners who had descended from families that had been in Norway for as long as anyone could remember. They had no children of their own, but had longed for one for the entirety of their 13-year marriage. They were also Nazi sympathizers and active members of the country's fascist party, the Nasjonal Samling, which had formed Quisling's puppet government.

On the morning that they collected their new child from the orphanage, Helga and Georg handed over 40 kroners, a state tax to be paid to the Reichskommissariat, in return for the required adoption papers. Then they collected their son, loaded him into their car and motored out of the city and into the hills beyond, to the valley of Sigdal and a big house on an ancient farm surrounded by forest.

The house they carried him into that day was quiet and cold. Its five bedrooms were filled with antique furnishings, and its twelve wood stoves could be fed with an endless supply of wood from the surrounding forest, protection against the cold that seeped through the thick lumbered walls. Helga and Georg placed their new son in the main sitting room, where friends and family soon gathered to welcome him.

To the guests who met him that day, his origin remained a mystery. And though they asked where he came from, none were ever told. Not everyone was so accepting of Georg and Helga's politics. Some were members of the Nasjonal Samling, while others belonged to the resistance Hjemmefronten. And so they spoke of other things and signed their names in a book of welcome for the boy who had just been rechristened Dag Skartum Åbye.

"The fair-haired one has behaved very well and made a good impression," Dag's adoptive aunt and newly appointed godmother wrote before passing the pen.

DAG HAD BARELY arrived at the Aabye manor when rumours began to circulate about his origins. He had been adopted onto an ancient farm situated in the Sigdal valley, which was populated by close-knit families who had lived in the hills and forests and farms since time immemorial. His arrival had been meant to solve a pending crisis of heredity. As the Aabyes' first son, he was in direct line to inherit one of the region's most coveted farms. But there were many in the valley who wondered if the child represented something more than what he appeared. Some wondered quietly if he had been the product of an affair between Georg and a woman from the capital. Others questioned openly whether he was a Lebensborn child. The occupation was already in its second year by the time Dag arrived. Many in the valley knew that the boy's adoptive parents were fascists, but they were just beginning to understand the lengths to which the Germans were going to "purify" the bloodlines. They knew the Nazis viewed Nordic blood as some sacred reservoir, falsely linking Germany and Norway together in an Aryan race myth that was rooted more in science fiction than in anthropology. The Nazis believed the Aryan people had originated from the island of Atlantis and had dispersed into northern Europe after Atlantis was wiped from the map. They did not understand that the people of Norway were in fact largely descended from neoliths who had migrated to the region from Africa by way of Europe and Asia a few thousand years earlier.

For more than 2,000 years, there have been farms in the valley of Sigdal, passed down through generations of families. The Norse gave the valley its name. They called it Sigmardalr, for the river Sigma (now Simoa), which snakes along the valley floor. For generations, the people of Sigdal have been known as the Sigdøling ("those who are related to Sigdal"). Culturally, they are not so different from other Norwegians who have lived over the hills in the neighbouring fjords and valleys for as long as anyone can remember. But just like the people in those neighbouring

Dag was roughly four years old at the end of the Second World War. Life at Hovlandsmoen remained uneasy for the Aabye family after the war. (Courtesy of Dag Aabye)

regions, the Sigdøling are an exclusive group, bound together by centuries-old traditions and relationships that keep them connected, not simply to the land they call home, but to each other. And though it is from the land that the Sigdøling inherited their name, to simply live in Sigdal has not always made someone a Sigdøling. In the past, some believed that to be Sigdøling was to carry the name of one of the many farms in the valley that have housed the same families for generations.

Even before the advent of modern DNA testing, many Sigdøling could trace their lineage all the way back to the Norse farmers who, after watching half their population perish during the Black Death, began recording their local history in written documents that survive to this day. In those early records the first reference can be found to a farm called Hovlund (from the Old Norse *hof*, meaning "pagan temple" or "place of worship," and *lund* for "land"). One of the oldest farms in the region, it is mentioned in texts that date from 1360, though the farm itself is believed to be older. It was a large farm even by 14th-century standards, and by 1615 its southern half had been subdivided and renamed Hovlund Søre. By 1882 Hovlund Søre was known as Hovlandsmoen and was annexed into the growing holdings of a local farmer whose descendants still owned it when Dag arrived.

Like all of Norway's ancient farms, Hovlandsmoen has long been considered a sacred asset to those who farm it—passed down like a crown through generations by the principle of primogeniture. Since the time of England's Tudor monarchs, the first-born legitimate son of Hovlandsmoen has held the right of inheritance to the farm. A farmer's birthright is so important to Norwegian society that the lineal ownership of the country's farms is protected by an ancient Scandinavian law known as *odelsrett*, which allows every member of a farmer's family to know exactly where they stand in the line of succession for any lands even remotely connected to their family history. The *odelsrett* is so far-reaching that few farms ever find their way to the open market.

On those rare occasions when entire bloodlines ran dry and farms were sold, they were most often bought by neighbouring farmers, who then passed them down to their own second-born. Often the second-born sons shed their family name and took on the name of their farm, linking themselves to their land for generations to come.

When he was adopted onto Hovlandsmoen, Dag Skartum Aabye was brought into a wealthy family that had acquired many farms. He himself was given a name that carried a connection to two separate plots of land: Skartum and Aabye. The story of Dag's adoptive family is one of dynastic legacy that traces back to 1838, the year a 50-year-old widower and wealthy farmer named Torstein Eken passed his family farm to his eldest son and purchased for himself one of the oldest farms in the valley, a 480-hectare mix of arable soil and forest that dated back to the Norse, who had named it Skartum, "a beautiful place." Eken changed his name to Skartum, remarried and began a new family. Upon his death in 1861, Torstein bequeathed Skartum to the eldest surviving son of his second marriage, the 19-year-old Andreas. Andreas was an industrious man who, 20 years later, leveraged his family's wealth to purchase what was then and remains to this day one of the most coveted farms in the entire valley—Hovlandsmoen. When Andreas died in 1921, his son Carl, who had already inherited Skartum in 1913, took control of Hovlandsmoen as well. For 10 years, Carl profited, like his father before him, from running two of the region's grandest farms. Then he died of a heart attack at the age of 46, leaving five young daughters and a large fortune.

Dag's adoptive mother, Helga, was the eldest of Carl's daughters. An heiress on paper at the age of 15, she required a husband of a certain social status and agrarian know-how in order to guarantee her future as the rightful inheritor of either Skartum or Hovlandsmoen. She found the ideal husband in Georg Aabye, the youngest son of a well-to-do farming family from a neighbouring village. Upon their marriage in 1929, Helga and Georg let go of their right to Skartum, passing it down to one of Helga's sisters, and chose instead to take Hovlandsmoen, a 1,400-acre rolling forest and pastureland that stretched from the Simoa river over a nearby hill and into a whole other valley. Hovlandsmoen comprised several log cabins for its workmen, two storehouses, two barns and two farmhouses, one of which was a truly magnificent white wooden manor that had been built by Helga's father and stood on a plateau overlooking the lone road that cut through the valley next to the Simoa river.

Through the first 13 years of their marriage, Helga and Georg worked tirelessly to make Hovlandsmoen one of the most productive farms in the valley. Georg maximized the land's wheat production while harvesting only a fraction of its lumber, choosing instead to nurture fresh seedlings in the hope that one day they would prove valuable to his heir. All the while, Helga redecorated the manor, filling it with priceless antiques. But while their wealth and prestige in the valley grew, something was missing from their farm—a child to pass it down to. Dag's arrival appeared to solve the couple's familial woes. For a while, things went well for the family of three. The farm was prospering even as the rest of the country suffered through the occupation.

Then the tide of war began to shift. Soon it became apparent to all in the valley that the Aabye family was on the wrong side of history.

SEVEN

ADOPTED SINS

You are not safe. We will kill you and we will burn your farm and your treason will be known.

—ANONYMOUS LETTER DELIVERED
TO HOVLANDSMOEN AT THE END
OF THE SECOND WORLD WAR

The war was nearly over by the time soldiers arrived at the farm. Dag wasn't yet four years old, but he was old enough to know not to get in the way of the men who slept in the barn on their way through the valley. It was April 26, 1945, a cold Thursday just two weeks before the German surrender, when 100 Waffen-SS soldiers, who were mostly Norwegian teenaged volunteers, were deployed just north of Sigdal to a nearby lake, in search of a weapons stash. Once there, the soldiers were ambushed in a four-hour crossfire skirmish that left an unverified number of dead on both sides. The Battle of Haglebu, one of the last of the war, was one of many clashes between Norwegian partisans and Norwegian traitors. Among the shots fired at Haglebu was one that killed a 21-year-old Norwegian Waffen-SS member who was executed by the partisans shortly after he surrendered.

These were the dying days of the war. In Germany, one and a half million Red Army troops had encircled Berlin and were engaging in street-to-street combat against children while Hitler hid out in the Führerbunker. In Oslo, the Reichskommissariat was losing strength quickly. Skirmishes broke out across Norway as local Resistance fighters escalated their attacks on Nazis and Nazi sympathizers. As German forces retreated south through Norway, they destroyed houses, barns and fields to slow the advance of Soviet soldiers coming into the country from the north. Approximately 50,000 people were displaced in the process, and many of them were forced to seek shelter through the winter of 1945 in huts, caves and mines.

As the war raged to its conclusion, Dag's parents found themselves living in an increasingly dangerous world. The Norwegian public was angry and exacting revenge against all who had collaborated with the Germans.

Two days after the Battle of Haglebu, news broke from northern Italy that Mussolini and his mistress were hanging from meat hooks in a Milan square. Dag and his parents sat holed up at Hovlandsmoen, listening to reports on the radio, alongside guests from out of town who had been unable to return to their home because of the growing threat in the region.

On the day of Hitler's suicide, Liv Imerslund, the Aabyes' guest, captured the sentiment at Hovlandsmoen when she wrote in the farm's guest book: "I wonder what the coming days and weeks will bring. Berlin is destroyed, the war between Germany and the Allies will probably soon come to an end. Will there be another war after this one? How will the world be afterwards? The air is full of questions in addition to all the rumours."

On May 7, the day Germany officially surrendered, 400,000 German troops remained stationed in Norway. For a brief moment, Josef Terboven, Reichskommissar for Norway, seemed intent on making the country the last bastion of the Third Reich. Then he took his own life, blowing up his bunker beneath the Norwegian royal palace. Soon German soldiers began surrendering to the Norwegian underground, while

British airborne troops dropped into the fields outside Oslo, bolstering the Resistance and arresting Nazi officers across the country.

Though the surrender had been relatively peaceful, the country remained deeply divided. Vidkun Quisling, whose name had become synonymous with treason, was arrested on May 9 and placed on suicide watch. Meanwhile, Norwegian police and partisans fanned out across the country, rounding up all those who had supported Quisling's puppet regime. The partisans were angry. More than 44,000 Norwegians had been arrested during the occupation, and 9,000 of those were sent to prison camps outside Norway. Many never returned. The retribution against Quisling's supporters was swift: 28,500 collaborationists were quickly arrested and slowly questioned.

The day after Quisling's arrest, a death threat was left on the porch at Hovlandsmoen. It bore the clumsy handwriting of someone trying to mask their identity. It wasn't the first time the Aabyes had received a death threat at the door, though the previous letters were always typed and addressed to Georg, and bore an Oslo postmark. This letter was different. This one had no stamp and had been hand-delivered to the door. It said that now that the war was over, all traitors would soon be shot and their houses burned.

Dag never knew anything about the letter. Helga and Georg shielded him from the threats as best they could, up to the point of their arrest for treason. Dag didn't remember if it was day or night or if it was cold or if he cried when armed men arrived at the house and demanded that his mother go away with them.

It was three days to his fourth birthday and four days since the end of the war. He remembered how quiet everything seemed before it all got loud. Soon Dag was scooped up in a housekeeper's arms and rushed toward the forest beyond the house. They were still running when a large truck came up the driveway. It revved loudly as it climbed the hill toward the house. Then there were countless voices, loud voices. Dag looked back at the house and watched as men with guns entered the barn and walked in and out of the house.

He doesn't remember whether he observed from a distance as the men loaded Helga into the back of their truck and then drove away. He doesn't remember whether the woman who carried him into the forest managed to keep him quiet or if she explained to him what was going on. He didn't realize, either, that deeper in the forest, his father too was being led away from his work at gunpoint into the back of a truck.

Though Dag's name was largely kept out of his parents' treason trials, those who lived in the valley at the time speculated that his adoption had been part of the Aabyes' crimes. No one could prove it, but many suspected that Dag's father was German. For 110 days, Helga and Georg remained separated and in jail. Dag spent the time living with Helga's mother on a nearby farm. His parents were still in jail when, just over five months later, Vidkun Quisling was executed by firing squad in Oslo.

A month later Helga and Georg were convicted of treason, but their lives were spared. Instead they were fined nearly the entirety of their net worth, but were permitted to hold on to their land. They paid the fine, collected Dag and returned home.

FOR THREE MORE years the threats continued. Dag was kept completely oblivious to all of it. He had his toys, and he had an imaginary friend, and though he often found himself alone on the farm, unsure where anyone was for days on end, he never felt unsafe. He didn't realize that beyond the confines of Hovlandsmoen, many children of the war were targets of state-sanctioned reprisals. Thousands of children were stripped of their citizenship. Some were branded as developmentally disabled and locked in institutions. Others were brutalized in the streets.

Though Dag's parents had paid their fine, they remained traitors in the eyes of many. By the winter of 1949, it was clear to both Helga and Georg that it was time to leave Norway.

EIGHT

ARGENTINA, 1949

Everyone is guilty of something, or has something to conceal. All one has to do is look hard enough to find what it is.
—ALEKSANDR SOLZHENITSYN,
QUOTED IN DAG'S JOURNALS

It was never clear to most people who tried to get to know him why certain portions of Dag's history were shrouded in an impenetrable mystery. He rarely spoke to anyone about his origins or adoption, and when he did, the story varied. Sometimes Dag claimed he had been found on the steps of a church. Other times he maintained that he had been left on the doorstep of the farmhouse where he grew up. On multiple occasions he said his father was a German U-boat officer, but most often his father had no backstory whatsoever. Those who tried to make sense of it often found themselves more confused for trying. His children, his ex-wife—none were sure what to make of where he came from because it was never clear, even to those closest to him, what he actually knew to be true.

As best as anyone could tell, Dag truly believed everything he said, even when the things he said were outright contradictions. I first understood this complexity on the road to Jasper, when Dag spoke of his childhood and adolescence, especially of the years he spent in Argentina after the end of the war. He described how at the age of eight he had been dropped off by his parents and left in the care of Germans who had arrived in the country at a time when Nazi stowaways were coming into Argentina via the ratlines that had been established by the government of Juan Perón.

There was a lot to digest in what Dag was saying. But it proved difficult because I wasn't sure whether he understood or accepted why his parents had emigrated to Argentina to begin with. His explanation was vague and omitted the fact that they had followed the exodus of Nazi war criminals, collaborators and sympathizers who had navigated their way to Argentina through a series of nefarious diplomatic openings that allowed Germans, Poles, Swedes, Spaniards, French, Italians, Croatians and Norwegians to escape postwar retributions.

Dag said his parents were farmers and times were tough in Norway after the war. One day, he said, they learned that farmland was cheap in Argentina, so they uprooted to the far side of the world, purchased a cotton farm and started over on a swath of land that was markedly smaller than Hovlandsmoen. In Dag's version the cotton farm was in a part of Argentina that was so remote there was no school nearby. And so his parents left him in the care of a German family who lived in a village several hours away.

Specific moments from his time in Argentina stood out in his mind, but that period of his life, as a whole, seemed somewhat blurry. Like everyone's memories, Dag's accounts of his past were accumulations of facts and observations, experienced in the moment yet corrupted by inference and reaction. But sometimes his concepts of truth omitted obvious facts. I believed it to be more innocent than anything else, a case, perhaps, of wilful ignorance—a natural method to avoid having to deal with facts that did not align with what he *wanted* to be true. His simplified understanding of his parents' history seemed crucial to his emotional survival, but it was ultimately detrimental to other people's attempts to understand who he was and what had happened to him.

One of Dag's cousins, a physician from Copenhagen named Kari Jørgensen, who had spent her childhood summers at Hovlandsmoen and who grew up enamoured of Dag, helped shape my understanding of how his mind worked when she told me: "There is a beauty to the way he sees the world that has been there for as long as I have known him. He may seem naive, but I think that he survives, mentally, through positive thinking."

Regardless of what Dag did or did not understand about his parents' treason, the threats to their lives or the reasons for their sudden flight to Argentina, it was clear to those who knew the family that his parents boarded SS *Belgrano* in the spring of 1949 not because they were crop farmers looking to test themselves in the cotton industry on the other side of the planet, but because they needed to get out of Norway for their own safety.

The particulars of their stay in Argentina have been lost to time. Much of the paperwork related to the arrival of Nazis and collaborators, including landing permits, was burned in the late 1990s by the Argentine government in an attempt to cover up the Perón regime's efforts to, as one German diplomat put it, "transplant the Nazi ideology to South American soil."

At the time of the Aabyes' departure for South America, the Perón regime was bent on creating an Argentina-led southern bloc to challenge the United States' hegemony in the Western Hemisphere. Perón, who began his rise to power in 1943, had been armed by Spanish ships loaded with German munitions. By 1944, when it became increasingly apparent that Germany was going to lose the war in Europe, the SS and the Peronists held meetings to discuss how to save Nazi men and women whose crimes were destined to lead them to the gallows after the war. Escape routes were mapped out via multiple countries (including Norway) to relocate a steady flow of Nazi refugees to South America.

On the same day that Helga Aabye stood on her porch reading a threat from the home front, U-boat *U-977* dropped off 16 of its crew on an island near Bergen, on the western side of Norway, then slipped under the water, only to reappear 99 days later off the Argentinian coast. The story of that U-boat's journey, along with that of another boat that escaped Allied detection near Norway and found its way to Argentina after the war, have long fuelled conspiracy theories that Hitler may have left Germany in the dying days of the war. The truth, however, is that the majority of the Nazis who escaped to Argentina did so using false names on board merchant ships and planes that trickled out of multiple European ports in the five years following Germany's surrender.

Georg and Helga were still in custody when Carlos Schulz, Perón's number one Nazi recruiter, arrived in Scandinavia to rescue as many fugitive Germans as possible. While in Oslo, Schulz managed to secure safe passage to Argentina for Nazis and Nazi collaborators who had been imprisoned after the war. Then he moved on to Stockholm and Copenhagen, to secure safe passage for many German soldiers and criminals who had fled to Denmark to escape the Allied advance in the final months of the war.

By 1949, the ratlines had been open for five years, offering temporary salvation to defeated Nazis and sympathizers in Europe. And though many who used them to slip away to Argentina did so to escape persecution or prosecution, others were guided by a twisted belief that on the far side of the world, a Fourth Reich could be built.

Dag knew quite a bit about the ratlines, but he wasn't convinced he and his parents had been funnelled out of the country through any of the channels that had been set up to save Nazis and their sympathizers. He truly believed they had gone to Argentina to try their hand at cotton farming. But he also understood that most of the people he got to know in Argentina were originally German. At times, I found when I pressed him for details of what had happened there, he would simply go quiet. He preferred to maintain a pleasant veneer over his time in that country, though his childhood neighbours back in Sigdal remembered him, when he returned, feeling as though he had been abandoned in Argentina.

For Dag and his parents, the journey from Norway in 1949 was long and fraught, filled with confusion and uncertainty. They left most of their belongings at Hovlandsmoen, unsure when it would be safe enough to return but certain that someday they would. They sailed first to the Canary Islands and into the old port of Santa Cruz de Tenerife, then onward to Buenos Aires.

There, they set up in Tigre, a section of the city that was home to many German immigrants and refugees and just a few kilometres from where Adolf Eichmann, the architect of the final solution and the "world's most wanted Nazi," was eventually arrested. Dag was eight years old and had vague memories of his parents going to meetings in the night and leaving him alone in the apartment for long periods of time. It wasn't until years later, when he read about the arrest of Eichmann, that he realized he and his family had been holed up in a veritable Nazi enclave within the city.

Georg told Dag early on during their stay that he wasn't to ask anyone anything. It was good advice, which Dag heeded when the family left Buenos Aires and moved deeper into the countryside. Dag's parents chose not to take him with them to their final destination, entrusting him instead to a group of Germans who had set themselves up in a lonely village next to the wild and sprawling countryside of Gran Chaco. He spent nearly two years living in a boarding house surrounded by strangers and with no sign of his parents, who were 300 kilometres away farming a piece of land so rugged and remote that Georg carried a Luger on his belt at all times. (Dag never quite explained why he needed the gun.) Dag's only connection to his home was in the books Helga and Georg left with him when they continued deeper into the countryside. As the months passed, Dag sometimes wondered if his parents had forgotten him, though Helga and Georg did send him letters. He wasn't the only parentless child in the house, but he was the only one who couldn't speak either German or Spanish, though he eventually learned enough Spanish to get by.

On the rare occasion he did see his parents, they would drive him to the mud-and-straw house near where the jungle and the arid lands meet. That's where their cotton farm was. While there he rode around on a horse named Petiso.

But he also did as his father instructed and tried not to ask questions, and he especially kept his distance from the armed men who would ride in from the rolling pasturelands that stretched west from the Paraguay River and spend the night in the barn.

The Aabyes' was a small farm in comparison with Hovlandsmoen. Their main struggle was clearing enough land to produce the required quota of cotton to keep the farm profitable. But the terrain was so rough that it could take an entire year just to clear an acre. Dag never stayed with his parents for long and was soon driven back to the Germans, where he found himself surrounded yet again by children from European cities he knew nothing about.

After two years, Norway became a distant memory. Some days, Dag couldn't even recall what life at Hovlandsmoen had been like. How the snow used to cling to the trees beyond his bedroom window, or how it felt to run his nails through the frost on the window, or the sound of a crackling fire next to his bed.

Then, one day, Helga and Georg drove in from the savanna in their Land Rover. They told him it was time to pack up his things and for the three of them to return to Norway. He didn't have much to say to them as they started the long journey home.

NINE

THE LONG FALL

Consciousness shapes reality.
—DAG'S JOURNALS

Early on a cold October morning in 2016, Dag woke to the familiar sound of the wind rustling through the cedar branches swaying above his bus. He turned on his headlamp and climbed out of the bed he had built out of plywood and foam in the back of the bus and shuffled toward the wood stove he had installed in the middle of the bus, which kept him warm in the night. He poked the coals and threw another log on the fire. Then he placed his kettle on the stove and tuned in to the four o'clock news. The morning airwaves were filled with stories of the ongoing siege in Aleppo and the growing unease over a potential Donald Trump presidency. Dag watched the log burn in the fire and waited for the water to boil, and when it did he made himself a cup of instant coffee. Then he tightened the laces on his boots, zipped up his jacket, grabbed his tuque and gloves and was off, running through the cold night and a fresh layer of frost and snow.

He was making good time on one of his favourite trails, an eight-kilometre loop, which he called "Adele" for the woman whose music he had never heard but whom he respected nonetheless thanks to the reviews he had read in the Sunday *New York Times*.

Four months had passed since I watched him bow out of the Death Race after running 49 kilometres in nine hours. He was already training for the following year's event and trying, as best he could, to head into the winter in peak physical condition. He had felt inspired by a story he read in the *Globe and Mail* about Ed Whitlock, an 85-year-old former teacher who had broken the record for the fastest marathon run anywhere on the planet by an octogenarian. Whitlock broke the record at the Toronto Waterfront Marathon earlier that month and earned international recognition for his feat. Dag had cut out some of the coverage and taped it into his journal as a reminder that he was not alone in his efforts to recast the way society looks at the elderly and what they can do. He had studied Whitlock's story well enough to know that the English-born road racer liked to train by running on the paved roads at a cemetery on the outskirts of Toronto. Researchers at the Mayo Clinic were analyzing how Whitlock was able to do what he did, one even commenting that "he's about as close as you can get to minimal aging in a human individual." Dag looked at what Whitlock had done—he completed the Toronto Waterfront Marathon in 3 hours, 56 minutes and 24 seconds—and saw it as something to admire more than as something to aspire to. Whitlock was a kindred spirit, an elderly citizen who was out there, every day, treading rubber—while also dying of prostate cancer.

The glow from Dag's headlight bounced through the night as he snaked his way deeper into the forest. He had been out on the trail for 30 minutes and was at least that far from the nearest human. He kicked up his pace as he rounded a bend and was making his way toward a steep switchback when he heard the flutter of wings. He had startled a grouse on the trail. The grouse lifted off from the ground and was trying to get out of his path when it flew right into his face. Dag didn't have time to react. He pressed his hands to his face and before he knew it he lost his footing and was falling fast, taking branches to the head and body as he veered off the trail, tripped over a stump and tumbled down a steep incline, bouncing off roots and rocks as his body crashed against deadwood and stone. He felt his shoulder crunch against the earth as he came to a stop, and heard his head crack against a rock. And then . . . nothing.

The blood from his face was cold and thick by the time he opened his eyes. He didn't know how long he had been unconscious, but it was still dark and his head was still bleeding. It didn't take long for him to realize that his arm was broken. He wiped his bloodied hair from his eyes with his one functioning hand. The pain was like a dagger stabbing into his mangled shoulder. It penetrated deep into the pit of his arm as he pulled his body back over the roots and stumps that had broken his fall. Back on the trail he stood still for a moment in the moonlight. He could feel himself growing weaker. Then he began to run once more, backtracking out of the forest. He knew he had to keep moving, but he had no idea where to go. He was too badly injured to return to the bus. So he trekked down toward Vernon. It would be more than an hour before he could see the city's lights.

BRENDA MORRIS PARKED her Nissan Altima in the dark. It was an hour before dawn on that cold autumn morning, and the 57-year-old server got out of her car and walked into the Roster sports bar. She flipped on a few lights behind the bar and was starting to make a pot of coffee when Dag wandered into the restaurant.

Dag was sometimes her first customer, and other times her last, too. He would often run through a hillside forest in the pre-dawn hours before heading into Vernon in the valley below and making his way to the Roster. Generally he would travel with just enough change for a cup of coffee and a breakfast sandwich. But sometimes he would show up with no money at all. Brenda would serve him anyway, and when he was done he would tell her: "Thanks from the bottom of my heart." Then he would poke around at his chest looking for his heart and pretend like he had lost it, before heading out to run up the hill and back to his bus.

Two decades had passed since she first met him. He had come into the bar, destitute and exhausted. Back then he hadn't yet started living out of the bus and had spent an entire winter sustaining himself on nothing but flapjacks, which he made out of the only two ingredients he could afford—flour and water. Broke, faint and on the brink of physical collapse, he had dragged himself into the Roster. His hunger was beginning to border on starvation. He could barely even make eye contact with the server as he asked, sheepishly, if he could have a coffee and charge it to a tab. He knew he could not pay. Brenda's brother, Rob, who owned the bar, took one look at him, poured him a coffee and brought him a club sandwich.

Dag vowed to repay the generosity by whatever means possible, and he had returned to the bar a few weeks later carrying a pair of 18th-century Norwegian skis—expensive antiques that he said had belonged to his mother. He left them next to the bar as a gift. For 20 years, the skis have hung on the wall near the pub's door, and for just as many years, the pub has been one of the only public spaces where Dag will sit stationary. As such, it became the place where even his children would sometimes leave messages, inquiring whether anyone had seen their father lately. At any given time there was at least one message for Dag, written on a Post-it note behind the bar. Sometimes those notes would be pressed to the bar for weeks, if not months, waiting until Dag came back. On quiet days, Brenda would sit behind the bar looking at a month-old Post-it and wonder if she would ever see the old man again. But whenever she started to question whether he was still alive, he would reappear. She would hand him whatever messages had been left for him and then he would disappear again. This time, though, was different.

She watched as Dag stumbled forward through the restaurant. She sensed something was wrong though she couldn't quite place it.

"Good morning, Dag. How are you?" she asked. He tried to answer but he wasn't making sense. Then, as he came closer to the light, she saw the blood on his face. Some of it was dry, but some of it was fresh, and he was cradling his right arm against his chest. His body was covered in mud. "You're hurt!" she yelled.

Dag winced as she sat him down. She turned on more lights and took a closer look at his injuries. His right arm was dangling out of the shoulder socket, and he had a large gash on the side of his head.

Brenda tied a makeshift sling, wrapped it around his dangling arm and supported it from his other shoulder. Then she wet a cloth and cleaned the blood from his face. It wasn't the first time she had cleaned him up after a spill on the trail. A few years earlier he had a run-in with a black bear. That time, Dag had leapt off the trail and knocked himself out, only to wake to the sound of the bear sniffing his backside. He hadn't broken any bones in that accident, though he had caused enough damage to his head and body to shut down his training for a few days. This time, however, he was seriously hurt.

"We have to get you to a hospital," she told him.

He shook his head. "I don't need a doctor to tell me that my arm is broken," he said. "They won't treat me anyway. I don't have a health card." It was hard to fathom how or why someone Dag's age, living the way he lived, would refuse what was essentially a basic human right in Canada. But he hadn't seen a doctor in 20 years, not since he had fallen out of a 50-foot pine tree while stringing Christmas lights at the base of SilverStar ski resort in the mid-1990s. Brenda insisted that if he wanted her help then he needed to let her take him to the hospital. She loaded him into her car and drove him to the emergency room. Soon a $1,300 X-ray showed that Dag's arm was injured badly enough to warrant surgery. He had dislodged his shoulder and broken the humerus bone. Dag smiled as the doctor explained the benefits of a $5,000 emergency surgery. As soon as the doctor was out of sight, Dag walked out of the hospital.

Days passed, and as he tried to navigate his life alone he soon learned it was impossible to survive as a one-armed hermit living in a bus on the side of a mountain. He could not chop wood, nor could he carry supplies or groceries in or out of the forest or dig the holes away from his bus that he used as latrines. Even the simple task of keeping the fire stoked in the wood stove was next to impossible. He was still bruised and battered when he ran back down to the Roster. Brenda looked at the fresh bruises on his body. Then she picked up the phone. There was no choice but to call one of his children.

For the better part of a decade, Dag's youngest daughter had been the only member of his immediate family who, from what I understood, checked in on him. Rarely, however, would he get back to her quickly. And when he did, it was to ask how she was doing with work, love and life. She lived in a small sawmill town near the edge of Alberta and just 30 kilometres north of the US border. It was 600 kilometres away from her father, but she was the only contact Brenda had for family in the area.

Dag's daughter was emotionally prepared for just about any phone call that ever came in from the Vernon area. This call caught her on the way to work, and she was soon listening as Brenda described her father's injuries and told her none of the clinics or the hospital in town would treat him unless someone agreed to pay the bill.

Brenda cut to the chase. "We don't know how to help him anymore," she said. She looked at Dag. His arm was still in the sling she had made for him days earlier. Winter was beginning to set in, and she wasn't convinced he would make it very long alone in the bus.

"Do you think he's well enough to travel?" his daughter asked.

"I think it might be his only option," Brenda replied.

For days, Dag put off making the trip. He didn't want to be a burden to his daughter. It had been nearly 20 years since they lived together. She had been with him through the darkest period of his life, shortly after his divorce, when she lived with him at the ski chalet that was his home. Then one day he came home and saw a For Sale sign on his property. His daughter moved out shortly after that. And though she always loved him, she tried her best not to think of him. Not out of spite, but because when she thought about him, she always ended up worried. Theirs was a complex relationship that sometimes benefited from and was sometimes harmed by the distance that needed to be bridged for them to meet. Now Dag was sitting in her kitchen, just a few weeks before Christmas, and looking incredibly fragile.

She took him to the hospital where she worked and asked a doctor to examine his arm. By then several weeks had passed since his fall and the humerus had started to heal, but Dag's arm was still misaligned from his shoulder, and the doctor told him that he would never regain full mobility out of that shoulder or arm. Dag was unperturbed by the news. He said he didn't need the arm for much. He had already begun to write with his left hand to avoid the pain that would flood through his arm when he tried to hold a pen in his right. As long as he could regain enough strength and mobility in the arm to swing an axe, he figured he could eventually get back to the life he wanted to live—alone in his bus. By late December, he could grip a mug in his right hand, but he still couldn't raise it off the table. Two months had passed since he had been able to really train. On Christmas morning he got out of bed and could hardly walk. His foot had been bothering him for days, though he hadn't told anyone.

His daughter noticed that he was limping. He had cut his right foot a few weeks earlier, when he was still living in the bus, and though the wound appeared to have healed, his entire foot was now turning red and had become painful to the touch. She rushed him back to the hospital. It took a while for the doctors to diagnose what was wrong with him. When they X-rayed his foot they could see evidence of multiple fractures, all of them old, none of which had healed properly. His foot looked like it could have been broken a dozen times. Dag told the doctor, however, that he had no memory of ever having broken his foot. But it wasn't the history of breaks that was causing the foot to swell. He had developed sepsis from not properly cleaning or caring for the recent wound, resulting in a bacterial infection that was so bad it was now threatening not just his foot but his life. His daughter was shocked and mortified.

"Do you know how lucky you are that you're here right now?" she asked him.

Dag didn't seem to understand that the infection, if left untreated, could poison his entire system. He was immediately placed on antibiotics.

It took several days for the pain in his foot to go away. Then, on the last morning of the year, he rolled out of bed well before dawn, pressed his foot to the floor and waited for the pain to set in. When it didn't, he rose to his feet and made for the door, laced up his boots, threw on his jacket and ran into the night.

New Year's came and went. January ticked by slowly. He ran as long and as hard as he could down the backcountry roads that rolled out from the town and over the great plateau that is the Rocky Mountain Trench. He could feel himself growing stronger with every passing day and every passing run. But he had been a mostly stationary object ever since his fall back in October, and he no longer possessed the endurance or the speed that he had before the accident. Then February came and he announced to his daughter that he would soon be going home. Back to the bus. Back to his trails and his journals and the life he had been living ever since the day he lost his home and was forced to seek refuge in a school bus parked on the side of a mountain.

His daughter didn't want him to stay indefinitely, but she was also hesitant to see him go. She tried to get him to accept his own aging, reminding him of the one thing he seemed unwilling to acknowledge: that if he had been alone in his bus he may well have slipped into septic shock and died. That even though he was strong and resilient, he was also fragile. She wasn't the first woman to try to persuade him to come out of the forest and grow old in the relative luxury of a clean house with heat and food. Barely a year had passed since his childhood friend and adoptive cousin, Kari, had come all the way from her home in Copenhagen to find Dag in Vernon. Near the end of her visit she asked him if he thought he would ever be able to settle down and live a normal life.

"What's a normal life?" he replied.

THE DAYS WERE getting longer, the late-winter sun hovering higher in the sky, by the time Dag got back to his bus. He dropped his bag on the ground, pushed open the door to his world and climbed inside. He built himself a fire and opened his journal to the entry from the day before his accident. Several months had passed since he was able to properly train. He noted the number of hours spent on the trails and the distance covered on his last run. Then he headed out to see how much time he had lost.

TEN

KINDRED SPIRITS

The first great thing is to find yourself and for that you need solitude and contemplation—at least sometimes. I can tell you deliverance will not come from the rushing noisy centers of civilization. It will come from the lonely places.

—FRIDTJOF NANSEN

But *why*? Why would a 77-year-old who had been given multiple opportunities to grow old in comfort and in the proximity of those who loved him choose instead to live alone in a dilapidated school bus on a mountainside? And why did he bother to keep abreast of society if he also did everything within his power to remove himself from the confines of any social contract?

These were just two of the unanswerable questions posed by my 72-year-old mother, whom I was visiting one day when my phone rang with a long-distance call from an unknown number.

My mother had been recovering from a bout of chemotherapy and was still trying to get back on her feet when I interrupted our coffee visit to pick up the call. It was late April 2018, and I was beginning to doubt that I would ever hear from Dag again. He had seemingly disappeared. We hadn't spoken since the previous fall, and I was struggling to locate him. I had left several messages at the Roster over the winter, but no one there had seen him in months. And now suddenly he was calling on a Saturday morning. My mother sat quietly listening to one side of what must have seemed a very strange conversation about bears and payphones, a school bus and my latest discoveries about tracking down the service records of Nazi soldiers stationed in Norway during the war. She watched as I scrambled for a piece of paper to write down a date and time one month later when I would meet my caller on a gravel road on the other side of the country. All I had to do was book a flight, rent a car and make sure I was on the right road at the right time.

My mother had many questions by the time I hung up, and she listened attentively as I shared the details, as I understood them, about Dag's life. What fascinated her most were the simplest questions of why and how. Why did he live this way, and how did he manage to do what he did? She was six years younger than Dag and she had been going to the gym three or four times a week for nearly 30 years. She was in good shape for her age until one day she wasn't. She was 70 when her knee gave out. Two years later she was diagnosed with breast cancer.

"Everyone I know, Brett, absolutely *everyone* my age has one ailment or another. We're all falling apart. Bad hips, bad knees, cancer, diabetes, heart conditions . . . Everyone's got something. This man has nothing?"

I told her about his broken arm. And about the blood poisoning that had set in after his foot injury.

She shook her head. "He must have remarkable genes," she replied.

I cringed. I didn't want to get into all the Nazi stuff with her at that moment. Instead, I simply said: "He views age as a state of mind more than an actual number."

She liked the sound of that. "Is he not aging as fast as the rest of us?" she asked.

"Well, he's able to run for 24 hours straight," I said.

She paused. "Surely he doesn't actually do that."

"Sometimes," I said.

"I didn't even know that was possible," she said.

I nodded.

There was a precedent for Dag's actions that I was just beginning to realize: a history of eccentric ultrarunners who had been misunderstood in life and remembered in death as historic curios. Chief among them was a legendary Norwegian named Mensen Ernst, whose unbelievable life ended on a hot January day along the banks of the Nile River in 1843. On that day, Ernst, arguably the greatest foot racer to have ever lived, leaned against a palm tree, draped a handkerchief over his face and is said to have succumbed to exhaustion and dysentery. He was believed to be 47 years old and had been running for nearly two months, covering 3,500 kilometres from eastern Germany to Jerusalem before veering west toward Cairo and then south, following the Nile in the hope of finding its origin. He had completed that run on very little sleep—resting in 10-minute intervals usually while standing propped against a tree—and even less nourishment—a biscuit a day and an ounce of raspberry syrup, if a *New York Times* account from 1879 is to be believed.

Legend tells that he was still on his feet propped up against that tree when some local villagers tried to wake him. When his body fell to the ground, they dug a hole and buried him on the spot where he had taken his last steps.

In life Ernst had attracted large crowds to see him run. As the *Times* reported in 1879: "The present interest in pedestrianism, manifested by the gathering of throngs of people to witness walking and running matches, was equally great in the early part of the century, but was then excited by the wonderful and almost incredible performances of one man. This was Mensen Ernst." Said to have been compact, muscular and squat, he ran in a white tunic and black trousers and wore a hat with a large plume. The first professional ultrarunner, Ernst found his calling while on leave from the merchant marine in London, when he placed a bet on himself to win a foot race from London to Portsmouth. He won that race in nine hours, then entered another, running from London to Liverpool in 32 hours.

Thus began a routine that saw him run into Paris, Berlin, Rome, Madrid and other cities, where he dared locals to bet against his ability to complete some absurdly challenging run. He would win the challenge and literally run off with their money. He drew some of his biggest crowds in Paris on June 11, 1831, when he departed Place Vendôme and set out for Moscow. He personally wagered 4,000 francs that he could make the 2,800-kilometre journey in 15 days. There was no one to meet him at the Kremlin when he arrived in just 13 days and 18 hours. His most daring feat, however, came when he was entrusted with documents from the East India Company that needed urgent transit from Constantinople to Calcutta, through some of the most inhospitable regions on earth. The East India Company gave him eight weeks to deliver the documents. Instead he completed the round trip in that time, running an average 140 kilometres a day.

Near the end of his life, Ernst befriended a Saxon prince who subsidized his ill-fated final race along the Nile as well as a German writer named Gustav Rieck, who chronicled Ernst's life in a book that came out while the runner was still alive. Rieck's book was loaded with mistruths that may or may not have originated from Ernst's own mouth. In Rieck's book Ernst is said to have been born in 1799 in the scenic port of Bergen, the son of a British naval captain and a Norwegian woman whose lineage could be traced all the way to Erik the Red. In the legend, Ernst's parents perished in a shipwreck on the North Sea, leaving the restless, rootless child to wander the fjords, later serving in the Royal Navy and seeing combat at the Battle of Navarino, the last significant naval battle to be fought entirely by sailing ships. None of that was true, however, as Ernst was actually born in 1795 in Fresvik, a small village on the shores of an inland fjord surrounded by mountains. He left the village at 15 to become a blacksmith in Bergen before relocating to Copenhagen for school. He left Norway, never to return, in 1813, and served aboard a British merchant ship.

As was the case with Dag, it was unclear where the reality of Ernst's story ended and the fabulism began. It was impossible not to draw parallels between the extreme exploits and often incomprehensible aspects that ran through both men's lives. The two shared innumerable similarities, not least their views on comfort and diet. Ernst is said to have guzzled wine by the bottle but abstained from food while he ran. Dag was much the same, though his toxin of choice was beer. He snacked on potatoes on longer runs but drank very little water. Ernst preferred sleeping on the ground outdoors, just as Dag did, both men being of the same mind—that it was better for the body.

Now largely forgotten to history, when he died Ernst was known as the great pedestrian and the itinerant foot racer. Today, he would have carried similar labels as Dag—homeless ultrarunner.

Dag had heard about Ernst, though he was never as enamoured with his story as he was with the tales of two other, far more famous Norwegian adventurers, Fridtjof Nansen and Roald

Amundsen. Extreme athletes of a sort, their stories inspired him from an early age when he first read both their memoirs. His fascination with each of them carried on into his adulthood, when he adopted elements of each man's philosophy into his own. His journals were themselves influenced by the work of Nansen, who once wrote that without his journals he would have been lost through much of his life.

Born in 1861 on the outskirts of Oslo, Nansen was a gifted skier and gymnast thanks to his flexibility and strength. But his greatest strength wasn't physical as much as psychological. On multiple occasions he proved himself capable of cross-country skiing nearly 100 kilometres in a single day. He preferred the quiet company of a lone dog on long expeditions and travelled as light as possible. A zoologist by training, he spent his student years aboard a Norwegian sealing vessel off the coast of Greenland, studying bears, seals and ice, and trekked overland 480 kilometres on skis from Bergen to Oslo to defend his thesis. That expedition was just a warmup for something far grander. He was 27 when he led what many considered a suicide expedition: to ski across Greenland. Nansen purposely chose to depart from the island's inhospitable eastern shore with his only possible destination a small fishing village on the opposite side of the island.

Explaining his rationale years later, he said he believed that a line of retreat is a snare, that you should burn your boats behind you so that there is no choice but to go forward. After two months on the glacial expanse that is Greenland, surviving temperatures as low as minus 45°C, Nansen and a team of six gained as much as 2,700 metres in elevation as they skied across the land, navigating their way around crevasses and cliffs, overcoming exhaustion and privation, before they emerged on the other side of the island.

Nansen returned to Norway a hero, entrenching the ski into the Nordic imagination. He inspired an entire generation of Norwegians, who began strapping on skis and pushing the boundaries of what was possible on snow and ice. Among his protégés was an athletic young man named Roald Amundsen.

Born on the outskirts of Oslo in 1872, Amundsen was an adventurer who studied medicine before taking to the sea. He was 25 when he first glimpsed the mammoth ice walls of the Antarctic coast. Back in Europe, he assembled a crew of six and purchased a 47-ton single-masted sloop, reinforced the ship's hull so it could withstand ice and sailed into Oslofjord to raise money and support for his ultimate goal, to sail the Northwest Passage. Unlike John Franklin, who had perished 50 years earlier searching for the passage with two warships and 129 men, Amundsen was determined to make the voyage with a nominal crew. It took three years for his ship to emerge in the Pacific. Amundsen and his crew returned home and were labelled the first heroes of the Kingdom of Norway, which had been formed after seceding from Sweden in 1905 while Amundsen was at sea.

But it was Amundsen's next accomplishment that made him every Norwegian's childhood hero. Capitalizing on the survival skills he had learned, largely from the Inuit in the Canadian Arctic, he set out for Antarctica and set up a base camp from which to launch the most gruelling endurance test of all time: the race to the South Pole. Unlike his English rival, Robert Falcon Scott, Amundsen overprepared for the expedition. He deposited food supplies along the first part of his route to the pole and draped himself in animal skins, which the Inuit had shown him were better than woollen parkas at keeping out the cold when wet. What's more, he arrived with a team of dogs and sleds to transport supplies, as well as skis. This was perhaps the most crucial difference between his expedition and that of Scott, who arrived in Antarctica with a team of Siberian ponies.

With four companions, 52 dogs and four sledges, Amundsen's team set out for the pole.

For nearly two months they navigated their way through clear weather until they reached their destination on December 14, 1911. They planted the flag of Norway and stayed for four days, eating a few of the dogs for strength, and then carried on back to their base. When Scott reached the pole a month later, he saw the flag and knew he had been beaten. Scott and his men perished while trying to find their way back to their own base.

Amundsen ultimately disappeared in a flying accident over the Barents Sea in 1928, while Nansen died of a heart attack in 1930. Years later, their exploits continued to be taught in schools to impressionable children like Dag, and the two men came to embody a prototype of Nordic masculinity and ingenuity. They also did more than anyone else to grow the sport of cross-country skiing in Norway and beyond. Skiing had long been Norwegians' winter sport of choice, but Nansen and Amundsen helped to popularize the use of skis for long-distance endurance tests.

The country was still in the throes of war when Dag got his first pair of skis, hand-crafted by a local carpenter who made wooden skis out of a shop next to his house. It was the end of an age, when Norwegian villages still had their own resident ski makers. They would cleave blanks out of logs, then chisel them down by hand until they achieved the desired form and camber. Then they would steam the tips and bend them before adding the toe straps. Many ski makers would then add their own personal artistry to the top of the skis and sell them to their neighbours.

Some of Dag's earliest memories were of leaving his skis by the door to the manor at Hovlandsmoen. There was no part of his parents' land that he could not get to on skis in the dead of winter. He would pack a lunch on his back and take off for the day into the forest, pushing himself as far as he could before turning around and making his way home. Some days he would be gone so long that by the time he got home the tracks he had made at the start of the day were gone, buried under a fresh layer of snow. Then he would go inside, stoke the fire in his room and read another page from Nansen's memoirs of survival in the High Arctic.

IT WAS MORE than just his nationality that bonded Dag to Ernst, Nansen, Amundsen and other Norwegian adventurers of the past. In the case of Nansen and Amundsen, Dag diligently studied them and emulated their obsessiveness in his pursuit of, and contentment with, solitude. Like them, he had a knack for masochistic thrill-seeking that crossed the line into addiction.

Scientists have been trying for years to isolate

the role that nature plays in the formation of extreme athletes. Some have posited that it can be traced to a genetic marker known as the DRD4 receptor. Dubbed the "adventure gene," one of the DRD4's variants has been controversially associated with thrill-seeking behaviour, like mountain climbing, skydiving, race-car driving and freestyle skiing. The DRD4 receptor controls the intake of dopamine by the brain, suggesting that it may be responsible for inspiring some athletes to risk their lives in the name of sport.

Researchers also now understand that dopamine is integral to the "runner's high"—a sense of euphoria that sets in either during or after a long run. The phenomenon is known to reduce anxiety and lessen a runner's ability to feel pain.

Dopamine may have explained, at least biologically, why Dag had gone from thrill-seeking freestyle skier in his youth to obsessive ultrarunner in his later years. But it did not explain how he went from teaching himself to ski to becoming the world's first extreme skier. Or how it was possible that one day in his mid-30s, he just got up and decided to run his first marathon without any training. Or how, nearly 40 years later, he was still setting personal bests for hours spent running in a year.

Dag didn't have much interest in the genetic and anatomical explanation for why and how he did what he did. He didn't actually believe that he had strong genes to begin with. He swore that he'd had a bad hip his entire life and that his longevity as an ultrarunner owed less to his genes and more to his daily exercise routine. He ran daily and nightly because it made him feel good, and if that was a result of a dopamine hit brought on by some genetic receptor, then so be it.

He didn't view himself as a thrill-seeking addict. In fact he didn't believe himself addicted to anything. He ran because he was driven by a personal philosophy that led him to try to push his body to the edge of possibility every single day. He acknowledged that he got a high every time he set a personal best, even if it was just for most hours spent trying to run a specific distance. But as far as he was concerned, there was no greater high than the one that came from a combined personal, psychological and physical accomplishment. He couldn't fathom why more people didn't view the world the same way he did. And he couldn't understand how or why so many seemed to struggle to put their phones down long enough to test their own limitations.

ELEVEN

LIFE ON SKIS

My wealth is not in what I have, but how I feel.
—DAG'S JOURNALS

All countries cherish their sporting celebrities, but no country elevates its skiers to the echelon of sport icons quite like Norway, where statues honouring the triumphs and accomplishments of dead skiers can be found in villages and valleys from the sport's cradle of Telemark in the south to the town of Lillehammer in the east and to the fjord of Trondheim in the north. Skiers in Norway are like footballers in Brazil and hockey players in Canada. And yet the ski represents something entirely unique in the Norwegian psyche. The ski helped humanity to explore and survive in Norway. There are even cave drawings to illustrate it. Nomadic hunters, flinging arrows at wild game, used prehistoric skis to glide over snow and ice and chase their prey into the Scandinavian Peninsula. For thousands of years after humans began populating the region, skis remained the preferred mode of transportation between Nordic villages. The Norse even prayed to a god of skiing, whom they called Ullr. From their rudimentary beginnings as carved planks bound to the foot by twisted birch roots to the modern composites with custom bindings, skis have remained central to Norwegian culture.

Part of that longevity is rooted in the country's ski brigades, which trained generations of soldiers to ski and shoot and gave rise to one of Norway's most popular sports, the biathlon. But part of it is also rooted in the fact that many Norwegians view their country, and specifically the Telemark region, as the birthplace of modern-day skiing. It was from Telemark that a 19th-century carpenter named Sondre Norheim emerged to become Norway's first national ski champion after winning a competition that was a mix of downhill and cross-country skiing. Norheim advanced what was humanly possible on skis when he designed his own bindings, which attached both the heel and the toe to the ski, offering the required stability to master the twisting and steep terrain that surrounded his valley. His Telemark binding was revolutionary, but it was soon overshadowed by the work of an Austria-based hermit who reverse-engineered a pair of Norwegian skis and further altered the bindings into something better suited to the steep terrain of the Alps. By the 1920s, the Rossignol, Völkl and Fischer companies had begun mass-producing hickory skis out of factories in France, Germany and Austria. Then things got really technical when the American aircraft engineer Howard Head started manufacturing skis from aluminum, fibreglass and other aviation materials.

But it was James Curran, an American bridge engineer who spent the early years of his career making conveyor systems to help load bananas onto ships in Honduras, who changed the sport forever when he took that conveyor technology to Sun Valley, Idaho, in 1936 and replaced the banana hooks with chairs. Thus was born the first chairlift. By the end of the Second World War, single- and two-person chairlifts were popping up on mountains all over the world. Suddenly people didn't have to hike up a mountainside with wooden skis on their back just for the thrill of a single descent. The bigger the sport got in Europe and North America, the less ownership the Norwegians had over any of it. Then along came Stein Eriksen.

It took Eriksen exactly two minutes and 25 seconds to re-establish Norway's image as a ski nation and to become the country's first postwar hero and poster boy for the 1952 Winter Olympics in Oslo. Eriksen, more than any other person, is often credited by journalists and ski historians with having brought about the global ski boom of the 1960s. And Eriksen, more than any other person, was often credited by Dag himself with having shaped the course of his life from the age of 10.

By the winter of 1952, seven long years had passed since the end of the war. The Aabye family had returned to Sigdal the previous summer, having been given the okay to come home by friends and family after the immediate threats to their lives had subsided. Dag spent the monthlong return journey by ship from Argentina in the company of the two people who called themselves his parents. He didn't resent his parents for abandoning him in Argentina, but they were strangers to him now. He spent as much time as possible above deck, ingratiating himself to the ship's crew by hammering rust off the deck and watching the waves crash against the hull as the ship steamed through the seemingly endless Atlantic. Spring turned to fall as they crossed over the equator and navigated north, rounding the Iberian Peninsula, cutting through the English Channel and making their way through Oslofjord. By Christmas 1951, the Aabyes were back at Hovlandsmoen and Dag was back in his childhood room, reacquainting himself with the feeling of frost on the window.

For the first few months back at the manor house, life was subdued. Then came February and the arrival of the Olympic torch in Oslo and the promise that the world's greatest skiers would soon descend on a 1,000-metre ski mountain not far from Hovlandsmoen.

On February 15, Dag stood with his mother next to the T-bar at the top of Norefjell Ski Resort, looking out in awe at the Olympic course that had been cut into the mountain's face. Spectators crowded along the sides of the course, with only a simple rope separating them from the Olympic skiers, who would shortly rocket down the mountain at breakneck speeds.

Helga led her son along the side of the course, searching for the perfect vantage point. She found it midway down the hill, next to a bend just before a sharp drop. Dag had never seen a non-wooden ski or a chairlift before. He leaned into the rope and flipped through a list of contestants. He recognized one of the names immediately: Henri Oreiller, the world's first Olympic downhill champion and a man reputed to be faster on skis than any car of the day. Branded "the madman of downhill," the Frenchman had essentially propelled the Rossignol brand to the front of the burgeoning ski market when he wore a pair to win the inaugural gold medal in downhill racing at the 1948 Olympics in St. Moritz. Oreiller entered the 1952 Olympics favoured by many to dominate once more. Dag looked on as the acrobatic Frenchman barrelled wildly down the mountainside. But it wasn't Oreiller who Dag and his mother had come to see. Like the thousands of others gripping the rope at the side of the course, the Aabyes were there to cheer for Stein Eriksen.

At the time Eriksen slid into the starting block for his Olympic run, downhill (or alpine) skiing was already a 60-year-old sport. It had come a long way since 1891, when Mathias Zdarsky, a Czech-born Austro-Hungarian hermit, nearly destroyed himself while trying to navigate a steep slope on a pair of cross-country skis he had ordered from Norway. Zdarsky, who is considered by many to be the father of alpine skiing, set about creating a whole new sport when he fashioned a steel binding to a pair of Norwegian-inspired skis to descend the Austrian Alps. Downhill skiing had evolved quickly from the teachings of Zdarsky, who tried to centre the sport on a set of awkward and primitive techniques that he concocted over the course of eight years spent largely in solitude in a small mountain village. His most significant contribution to the transformation of cross-country skis into downhill skis was a metal plate that was fixed to the top of the ski by a hinge, with straps that wrapped around the boot and kept the heel down thanks to a loaded spring. Having created the first true downhill skis, he began codifying the way they should be used and wrote the first textbook on alpine skiing. Instead of poles he used a long stick with barbed ends. This served as both balancing pole and a sort of harpoon, which Zdarsky used to spear the snow and pivot around in a snowplough turn. He packed his book with detailed instructions on how to do all this, and abhorred anyone who deviated from this style.

He was 49 years old when he organized what is considered the first alpine ski race, on March 19, 1905. Zdarsky set the rules of the race, as well as the course, fixing the gates in a serpentine pattern, forcing contestants to ski in what was essentially a slalom style. Zdarsky won the race but soon lapsed into obscurity. Nevertheless, he had planted his ski into the psyche of the Alpine nations. By 1952 and the Winter Olympics in Oslo, the Norwegian people were struggling to reclaim ownership of skiing as both a cross-country and a downhill sport, which is why the Norwegians had come out in droves to see the young Stein

Eriksen in what would become one of the most famous gold-medal runs in Olympic skiing history. Dag just happened to be on the sidelines watching the moment that skiing went global.

The opening ceremonies had barely begun when the 24-year-old Eriksen kicked out of the starting gate. He was largely unknown to the world, but in Norway he was already regarded as a fierce competitor: an Oslo-born son of an Olympic gymnast who had taught himself to ski and who was faster in the downhills than even the best of the best coming out of the mountainous Telemark region, where the world's greatest skiers had come from since the mid-16th century.

Eriksen was an unconventional racer who would turn his shoulders square to every gate while carving his skis in the opposite direction. He had trained primarily in Norway, while the rest of the Olympic field had trained together in the Alps. The competition among postwar European nations was fierce. Each country dispatched chemists to help blend the fastest ski waxes in order to give their nation's representatives the best chance possible on the Norwegian snow. The Austrians and the French were favoured for victory, and there weren't many people outside Norway who thought much of Eriksen's unorthodox style, which made him look completely out of control.

Dag couldn't see the starting block from his viewing point, but he could hear the crowd roar as Eriksen started his descent. Then came the sound of the Norwegian's skis carving into the icy crust of snow as he propelled himself around the first gate and then the second. Soon he was travelling upwards of 130 kilometres an hour, fast enough to drop nearly six metres in elevation each second. By the time he dropped into Dag's sightline he was stretched out into the apex of a turn, channelling the equivalent of one G-force into the edges of his skis. Then he rolled his weight and put everything into the opposite direction dropping over a knoll. For a moment Dag could hear no sound coming from Eriksen's skis because the man was literally flying. Dag never saw him land. All he heard was the roar of the crowd, followed by the sound of steel grinding into ice below. The whole run was over in two minutes and 25 seconds. Stein Eriksen secured the country's first gold medal in giant slalom and quickly replaced Oreiller as the most recognizable skier on the planet.

THAT NIGHT, DAG sat on his bed and looked out his window. The moonlight ricocheted off the snow-covered field and illuminated the forested hill in the distance. He was already visualizing the race track he planned to cut through the forest come morning. He got up early the next day, fetched his cross-country skis from the barn and set out with a vision of becoming the world's next greatest skier.

The sun was just beginning to crest over the hills when Dag set out into the woods to test himself on his own giant slalom course. He spent the better part of an hour slogging his way uphill, navigating around downed trees and errant boulders, until he reached a lookout that seemed as good as any to use as his starting block. He was far enough from home that his parents couldn't possibly make out what he was about to do.

He gripped his poles and looked down at the edges of his wooden skis. They had no metal attached to them, nothing whatsoever to carve into the snow. They were designed just for smooth forward movements. He didn't know much about the sport, but he knew that the skis on his feet weren't equipped to race downhill, nor to twist and turn around trees and boulders. But he was determined to do as he had seen at the Olympics. Then he pushed off and began gathering speed, successfully rounding the first tree and then the second. But suddenly he was going too fast and before he knew it he had lost control and was careening over boulders and brushing his body against tree after tree, clipping branches with his face, legs and torso. He was still somehow upright as he rocketed out of the forest and into a clearing, heading fast toward a wide gap in the pasture fence. There wasn't much room for error as he streaked toward the gap.

He was going far too fast to even notice that his father was standing by the fence. Georg watched as Dag blasted through the gap, narrowly missing one of the posts, before crossing the tips of his skis and catapulting head over heels into the snow. Dag pulled his face out of the snow and looked back to admire the tracks he had cut through the fence and into the trees beyond.

"Are you trying to kill yourself?" Georg asked.

The two stared at each other, Dag waiting for his father to drag him home to be chastised by Helga. Dag had already begun to fear his mother's reaction to pretty much everything he did.

"Don't let your mother see you doing this," Georg said. "Your grandfather planted those trees and built that fence."

Georg walked back toward the house, and Dag headed back into the forest to test his luck again and again. Before long, Georg booked a trip to Austria to buy Dag a proper pair of alpine skis straight out of the Kneissl factory in the Alps.

For the rest of that winter, Dag spent a portion of every day on his new skis. When he wasn't teaching himself how to race down his own manmade pistes, he was practising his footwork from a stationary position, trying to mimic what he had picked up from having briefly seen Stein Eriksen racing with his boots pressed together. Then Dag got to work on his first ski jump. He had read that every Sunday at one, Eriksen would stop whatever he was doing and execute something that he called the swan-dive front flip. Eriksen made the front flip look easy, even though it wasn't. Soon Dag was launching himself down the steepest slope he could find, right next to the barn, just a few metres from the only road that passed through the valley. Cars and buses would routinely stop while passing by the farm to catch a glimpse of Dag as he pushed himself off from the barn, down a steep hill and into a snow ramp that would spit him into the air at upwards of 20 kilometres an hour. The crashes were hard and spectacular, but so too were the landings. He was still young, but he was already on his way to becoming the world's first extreme skier.

All he needed was to get away from the farm.

TWELVE

LEARNING TO RUN

He was my friend, we told each other secrets.
We understood each other better than anyone.
I wasn't surprised when he left. He had to leave.

—GUNHILD BAKKE, DAG'S COUSIN

Helga Aabye was in a bad mood. It seemed to all who knew her that Helga was always angry at her adopted son for one thing or another. But on this particular day no one, not even Dag, was sure what he had done to set her off. He burst into the kitchen looking for something to eat and suddenly she was shouting and he was scared and nothing between them was ever the same again.

"You're nothing but the son of a Nazi whore," she screamed.

Dag was speechless and confused. He stood with his back against the kitchen wall, trying to understand what had just been said. No one had ever told him that he was adopted. He had no recollection of the orphanage in Oslo, and the only parts of the war that he could recall with any clarity were those moments when he had been filled with fear. Like when the phone would ring with a warning and the family would hurry outside and into the forest.

Dag lowered his eyes as Helga recoiled and covered her mouth. He had heard talk at school of *tyskerunger* (German brats) and of their traitorous mothers, *tyskertøser* (German whores). But he had never seen any of them in real life. He didn't want to, either. He knew enough about the war to know that the children were hated, as were their mothers.

Dag was still trying to make sense of what had just been said when Helga crouched down, placed her hands on his shoulders and held him firmly. "I'm sorry," she told him. "I'm so very, very sorry."

For days her words kept running through his mind. He didn't feel comfortable asking his mother for more information, and his father was away at the time. Then one day while he was playing alone next to the barn he saw his uncle Petter pull up to the house. Dag went over and helped him unload some tools from his truck. Then he told his uncle what Helga had said.

"How can I be a *tyskerunge*?" he asked. "I grew up here on the farm."

Petter looked at him, confused. "Did no one ever tell you the truth?" he said.

DAG DIDN'T WANT anyone else to know what Helga had told him. So he buried his questions along with his feelings and didn't speak about any of it for years. But from the moment Helga screamed at him in the kitchen, their relationship was severely altered. A distance grew between them, all through his adolescence. They quarrelled about everything, including his girlfriends, his clothing, his dreams and aspirations and also his grades. But the root of the conflict was always the same. She wanted him to be someone he was not. And because of that, he never really felt accepted at home. He ran away multiple times through his teenage years. Sometimes he would hide out in one of the log cabins at the far side of Hovlandsmoen. One time he slept on top of the laundry machine at a friend's house. Another time he caught a bus and went several hours away. It was always just a matter of time, though, before he ended up back in the cold old manor. He ran away so often that by the time he was 13, his parents had decided to send him away, enrolling him in a private boarding school. They hoped the distance and the strict schooling would make him more conformist. It didn't. Neither did a two-year stint in the Norwegian military that followed.

From the outside, it seemed to many in the valley that Helga and Dag almost hated each other. Their relationship was so bad that even Helga's sisters questioned whether Dag had been the product of an affair between Georg and some other woman. After all, Dag looked a lot like his adoptive father. They were both tall and thin, with high cheekbones and eyes that seemed to disappear in the sun. This theory helped explain the contempt Helga often showed the boy she had once vowed to raise as her own. She disapproved of so much he did, but mostly she felt that he was never grateful for the life she had given him when she brought him into her world.

Dag's friends at the boarding school remember him as a quiet kid who never spoke of where he had come from and rarely went home during holidays. They also remember him for what he did one February morning in 1958 when no one else was around. Sixteen-year-old Dag woke in his dorm room to the sound of breaking glass. He leapt from his bed and peered between the drapes to see that his school was engulfed in flames. Dag stripped his sheets from his mattress, tied them together and lowered himself out of his second-storey window. Acting on impulse, he ran toward the fire, climbed onto the roof of a breezeway and tossed and kicked snow from the roof onto the flames below. He was still up on the roof when three fire trucks arrived and took over.

It took several hours to extinguish the blaze. The next day's newspaper told the story of how a lone boy had slowed the fire long enough to save part of the school. The newspaper branded Dag a hero.

Dag was never a strong student, but from an early age he had been a superior athlete. He would often walk around the halls of his school on his hands and could even go up and down stairs while standing on his hands with his school bag balanced on his feet. He was obsessed with fitness. Back at Hovlandsmoen, he would work out by the barn using a homemade barbell, the ends of which he ran through the centre of tree stumps. Helga and Georg didn't care much for any of it. They thought he was a rudderless showboat.

"They wanted him to be something he was not," his cousin and childhood friend Gunhild Bakke would later recall. "They did love him, in their own way. But he was so different. The more they pushed, the more distant he became."

From the moment Dag arrived at Hovlandsmoen his adoptive parents had intended for him to inherit the farm. But he never showed any interest in any of it. Later, they tried to push him to become a lawyer or a doctor. But his grades were nowhere near high enough to get him into medical or law school. They feared something was wrong with him, so they made him take an aptitude test. He was a smart kid; he just wasn't interested in any of the things they were interested in. Whatever he lacked in grades, he made up for with his physical prowess, earning a coveted spot at a gymnastics institute near the Danish-German border.

Dag was 18 years old when he enrolled at one of the best-known schools for gymnasts anywhere in the world. It was 1959, and every day he spent in Denmark felt like a foreign adventure. He would train six days a week while simultaneously studying everything from social studies to weightlifting. Sometimes, on his one day off each week, he would jump on a bus and cross the nearby border into West Germany. The scars of the war were more than a decade old by then, and the northernmost state of West Germany was bustling. The British, who had occupied the territory in the years after the war, had helped to rebuild it, as had the 860,000 people who had been forced into the region by postwar migrations. But traces of the war could still be found on the faces of the broken men and women of the previous generations.

Ever since the day that Helga had called him a *tyskerunge*, he had struggled with the thought that his real father had been a German soldier. It made him question the nature of his own existence. At times he wondered whether he himself was the result of a Nazi war crime or the product of a German-Norwegian love affair. He had never bothered to ask Helga any questions after that day when she had screamed at him in anger. He assumed that his biological father had been killed in the war like so many others. He sometimes wondered if his father had been captured and killed by the Home Front, shot and burned by the advancing Red Army, or worse: drowned at sea in a U-boat. But the more time he spent along the border of Denmark and Germany, the more he wondered whether his father had perhaps survived it all and made it back to where he came from before the war began.

When Dag's term in Denmark was complete, he returned to Hovlandsmoen. But a lot had changed in the intervening year. Georg was over 50 now, and though he still looked young, he felt old and was eager for Dag to start taking over more responsibility at the farm.

One day, not long after he had returned home, Dag helped his father prepare logs for transport down to the river. He watched as his father slowed his pace and asked: "Who am I supposed to leave all of this to if not you?"

"This is your home," Dag replied. "I don't want it."

It wasn't long before Dag left the farm once more, this time for the Norwegian army. He spent hours standing sentry for the King's Guard and days criss-crossing the Norwegian countryside as a member of the ski brigades. He and his fellow soldiers would rise to the sound of a whistle in the middle of the night, made to go outside into the cold and sprint on skis through the forests and hills, moving fast toward the Swedish border and the rising sun. Dag, ahead of the pack, would launch his body into the snow, line his sights on a target, calm his breathing, and fire. Dag was stronger at skiing than he was at shooting. Then he would get back on his skis and make his return trip to the barracks. He was never quite sure just how far ahead he was from the rest of his brigade until he heard gunshots echoing behind him.

He excelled in the military, though he never progressed beyond private and never saw any combat. His strength, flexibility and endurance made him stand out during drills and war games. When summer hit, Dag quickly transitioned from top-tier biathlete into the Norwegian military's top pick for an international obstacle course. Soon he was competing against soldiers from Sweden, scaling walls five metres high, descending into pits three metres deep and navigating a balance beam and a low-hanging mesh of barbed-wire fencing.

There was a familiarity to the army, a kinship among the soldiers that made Dag both comfortable and uncomfortable at the same time. He spent six months training with British special forces (SAS) and served under a former Norwegian commando who was known as one of the "heroes of Telemark" for having knocked the Germans out of the race to build the first atom bomb by sabotaging a heavy-water plant during the war. "You're a son of a bitch," the officer told Dag. "But if we have a war I want you right beside me."

Dag was 21 years old, honourably discharged from the army and back living at the farm when he had one final blow-up with Helga. He had recently broken off a relationship with a girl whose social standing Helga didn't approve of. Then he got into a fight in a hotel restaurant at the base of Norefjell. Dag wasn't even sure how he ended up in the dispute. All he knew was one moment he was eating his lunch and the next moment he was lying on his back on a table with a middle-aged man towering over him and shouting into his face. Dag didn't bother to fight back because even after two years in the military he didn't really consider himself a fighter. He just rolled off the table and out of the crowded restaurant. When Helga heard of the altercation second-hand she told Dag he was an embarrassment to her family. She didn't even bother to ask what had happened or whether he was okay. Her response angered him more than anything that had ever happened between them in the past. So he left the farm for good, without even saying goodbye.

There was no note announcing his departure. Dag left no tracks, no trail through the snow for anyone to follow. His possessions sat preserved in the drawers of the desk and dresser in his bedroom. Every ski he ever owned was still in the barn, along with the Vespa he had ridden up to Norefjell, where he was running his own ski school, leading kids half his age down the same slope where he once watched Stein Eriksen win Olympic gold.

Dag had run away enough times over the years that it took a while for Helga and Georg to realize that this time he wasn't coming back. They checked the usual place first—the small cabin in the forest on the far side of Hovlandsmoen. It had been his getaway throughout his teenage years. But there was no sign of him there. No sign of him anywhere.

Helga quickly contacted the Salvation Army, hoping to enlist their investigative services to locate her son. But not even the Salvation Army, known for its capacity to find people almost anywhere in the world, was able to trace his movements. It wasn't that he was in hiding, or that he had worked particularly hard to cover his tracks. He had simply left the country without telling anyone. He had packed all that really mattered in his life into a canvas backpack, boarded a train to the port city of Bergen and caught a ferry out of Norway, traversing the North Sea to Newcastle before heading north for the Scottish Highlands. He had heard of a peak there called Cairn Gorm, a windswept summit populated by roaming reindeer that had recently become one of Britain's few ski resorts with a functioning chairlift. Once there, Dag purchased some ski gear, went to the resort's ski school and offered his services as an instructor. It didn't take long for the people running the school to realize that he was the most talented skier on their hill. They offered him a job and he started to teach. He didn't say much to anyone about the world from which he had come. And when people asked, he would simply say that he had been orphaned at a young age and had no real family. There wasn't much else he wanted to share.

THIRTEEN

GOLDFINGER

*You can't stand still just because
the world is burning.*

—DAG AABYE

The sky was red and ominous, marred by a thickening veil of smoke that blocked out the sun and cast everything in orange and grey as I cut across the Canadian Rockies on my way to find Dag. The BC backcountry was ablaze with more than 500 wildfires. I was coughing up phlegm and thankful for the purified air coming out of the vents inside my rented Chevy. It was August 2018, nearly three years since my first encounter with Dag. Myles and Derek had long since moved on with their lives, but I had once again abandoned mine to fly across the country and reconnect with the old man in the forest.

I was no longer searching for him just out of journalistic curiosity. I was looking for him because at some point along the way Dag had become my friend. He had gone from being someone I longed to explain to someone I wanted to understand. There was a magic to his outlook on life that I wanted to explore even if I never got the chance to tell his story. He had no interest in the trappings of modern society and was so in tune with his place in nature that it sometimes seemed as if he had more in common with the animals of the forest than he did with the rest of humanity. And yet he was a renaissance man, in his own way. He embodied an aspect of the renaissance tenet that "a man can do all things if he will." His formal education may have ended in a gymnastics school, but he was one of the best-read people I had ever met. He was an artist. His trails were his easel, his body his brush. He was underappreciated by those who didn't like his lifestyle, but like any artist of any repute he had a way of challenging people's perception of their world. He was determined that through his actions he could redefine our collective concept of aging.

There was a romance to his lifestyle that sucked me in, even though I knew it was rooted in personal tragedy. I admired him because although he was damaged he was not broken. I had begun to piece together elements of his life's journey through conversations with long-lost friends and estranged family, many of whom had not seen him in decades. And yet the more I learned about him, particularly about his relationship with his family, both in Norway and in Canada, the less I felt I understood him at all. And I was getting the sense from others that no one else really understood him either.

I had struggled just to get to him on this particular visit. The province was ablaze and clouds of smoke were beginning to stretch all the way from the Pacific Ocean to the prairies. The ashen sky was most dense in central BC, causing flights to be cancelled and passengers to be diverted hundreds of kilometres to land in Edmonton and Vancouver. I landed in Calgary, rented a car and began a 900-kilometre drive through the BC Interior. I had ventured in his direction on this particular trip partly because I was worried about him and partly because I had been trying to get him onto a plane back to Norway in order to help him solve the question of his origins.

The smoke was causing problems along the Trans-Canada Highway, slowing traffic and forcing me to take a circuitous route south through the Crowsnest Pass, which cuts through the Canadian Rockies before veering north along the Continental Divide. It took me two days of solid driving to navigate my way to Dag. Every time I stopped for gas or stepped out of the car to stretch my legs, the smell of smoke would hit me and begin to irritate my lungs. Public health officials were recommending that everyone stay inside and avoid physical exertion in the smoke. I understood why. But I also knew that Dag would be out there, keeping pace with himself in the forest.

I had last heard from him two weeks earlier. He had begun to call me whenever he found himself in the vicinity of a payphone. He liked to ask me what I thought of the latest news in the world. Then I would ask him how he was doing and he would share stories about the recent animals he had seen on his trails. Often, he would end his stories with an unexpected comment about some new injury. There were so many injuries, I struggled to keep track. He had been hit by a vehicle—twice—since the last time I had seen him. The first time he had been walking through a parking lot on his way to get food. The second time he had been running along the shoulder of a busy roadway, sandwiched between a guardrail and the road, when he had been clipped by a truck. He said the impact caused him to spin and fall over the guardrail. He said his arm was dangling from its socket again and he was starting to drop his coffee mug while drinking because his hand would give out and he would lose all strength. Then the fires set in and his calls became fewer and further apart. That's when I decided to fly across the country to see him.

I had last seen Dag four months earlier, when I flew into Kelowna and drove an hour north before veering east up Silver Star Mountain, then ducking left onto a gravel road and making my way toward a firepit in the forest that I knew he liked to use as a lookout. But this time was different. There was no point in navigating my way to one of his firepits because there was a fire ban in place across BC, and I had no idea where to look for him aside from his bus or the sports pub in town. I had never actually seen his bus, but I was pretty sure that I could find it on my own.

I was slowly twisting up an old gravel road a kilometre or so from where I believed his bus was parked when suddenly his slim, slow-moving figure began to materialize through the haze that blanketed the road. He was coughing hard yet chugging forward. He was on his way out for a run while everyone else sat shuttered inside, protecting their lungs. I pulled off the road, stepped out into the haze and shouted in his direction. He was happy to see me.

Minutes later we were sitting in the car with

the windows closed and the recirculated air pumping out of the vents. Dag struggled not to cough as I struggled to explain to him how I had flown across the country to float a hopeful idea to him.

"I think if I can get you back to Norway, I can help you find the graves of your biological parents," I said.

He hadn't been back to Norway in 26 years, and though he had thought about returning several times he never had the money or the documentation to make it happen. His previous passport had expired in the early 1990s, and he no longer had any valid photo identification. He had fallen off the radar of the Norwegian government 25 years earlier and he wasn't fully on the Canadian radar either. He kept his old passports hidden in a compartment under the floor of his bus, mixed in among newspaper clippings, old headshots from a two-year stint as a movie extra in London and postcards and letters from people he had known a long time ago. The long-expired passports, coupled with an old baptism certificate that he kept in a binder in a Rubbermaid bin on the driver's seat in the bus, were the extent of his official ID. He had no documentation to prove that he had been living in Canada legally ever since being invited here by the founders of Whistler Mountain to help open up the new ski hill back in 1965. He had no proof of permanent residency, and as a result, he had been warned by one government official after another over the course of the last 25 years that if he ever left the country he probably wouldn't be allowed back in. Despite not being able to prove his status, he managed to collect an old-age pension courtesy of the Canadian government and had kept out of trouble by living a simple life largely alone and off the grid.

"If you get flagged in a system as having been here illegally for 50 years, I don't know what will happen to you," I told him.

He listened and coughed and coughed and listened. He wasn't completely aware of how automated everything had become in the years since he last got on a plane.

He said the first few times he came to Canada, he did so legally. Around 1968 he crossed the border in the trunk of a Pontiac. But he said he had crossed the border multiple times since then and never had any problems. He had been stateside on photoshoots for ads for Kodak film, Fujifilm and a few cigarette brands. He said he had done quite a bit of modelling at the time. I had no idea what to do with that information, but I was starting to think that trying to take him back to Norway was a bad idea.

We sat in the car looking at the crimson and

grey air on the other side of the windshield. The hood of my rental was covered in a powdery residue that had clung to the paint as I cut across the province circumnavigating the fires. We weren't really talking. Then Dag reached into his small backpack.

"What's in the bag?" I asked.

He was carrying a couple of changes of clothes and a few rations of food. He said he wasn't sure where he was going because he didn't know where he could go to get to cleaner air. He had heard on the radio that the air quality in much of the province had become the worst on the planet.

"They say it's like smoking a couple packs of cigarettes a day right now," he said. His lungs were irritated, and his eyes were slightly inflamed. He didn't complain about any of it, but it was clearly having an impact on him. His bus offered protection from the rain and the cold, but it did nothing to filter the air.

"I want to show you something," he said. We got out of the car and walked into the forest toward one of his favourite lookouts. I had been there on a previous trip, when we stood in a clearing on a hillside looking out at the mountains in the distance and the valley below. But now there was nothing to see, just a wall of grey.

"I've never seen it this bad here before," he said.

The closest he had ever seen was in London. He had arrived there at the tail end of 1962, right after the infamous London fog killed 700 people in one particularly smoggy week. The smog that winter had been so palpable that those who lived through it said it tasted like metal in their mouth. There was no taste to the fog by the time Dag arrived, but he remembered how walking through the streets of Soho was like walking through soup. By contrast, the air we were breathing in now tasted of peat and ash. We were still standing at that lookout as Dag started reminiscing about his days in London. He said he had dated the daughter of a *Daily Telegraph* typesetter, lived his life as if it was set to Dave Brubeck's "Take Five" and witnessed Beatlemania and the rise of the Rolling Stones.

He said he had seen the Fab Four in the flesh at the height of their fame. It was July 6, 1964. He had been caught in the throng of 12,000 screaming teenagers who lined the street from Piccadilly Circus all the way to Leicester Square for the world premiere of *A Hard Day's Night*, a film that many of his fellow movie extras had been in, though not Dag himself, because he didn't have the right hair.

"People were passing out they were screaming so hard," he said. "There was no way to get out."

He didn't speak much about the celebrities he had met, unless he was probed. But he was in a reflective mood as we returned to my car, although the stories he told were disjointed and lost in both time and space. One moment he was talking about the time Pierre Trudeau had given him a piece of unsolicited advice at the Whistler lodge. The next moment he was telling me about a card game on a London soundstage with Ursula Andress, whom he described as always being in a bathrobe. "She gave me some practical advice," he said. "'It's better to be a star in a nothing movie than to be a co-star in a big movie. If you are a co-star too many times, that's all you'll ever be.'" He said he had been carrying that advice with him ever since. Sometimes listening to Dag felt a lot like watching *Forrest Gump*. His life seemed to be riddled with encounters with famous people and tales of incredible feats, but they were often hard to believe and were so all over the place that it was difficult to string them together in my own mind with any sort of narrative through line. There were so many stories, about Enzo Ferrari and Donald Sutherland and Michael Caine, though they didn't seem to have a moral. Then there were the stories about Sean Connery. "Connery was different from the rest of them," Dag said. "He wasn't a nice guy playing tough, but a tough guy playing nice." Then he started coughing again and for a while it seemed he wouldn't be able to stop.

It took several hours of sitting side by side with Dag, driving through smoke listening to him narrate his journey through the 1960s for me to be able to make much sense of how and why he had gone from being a vagabond ski instructor in Scotland to a movie extra in some of the biggest films produced in the early and mid-1960s before hightailing it to Chile and then to Canada, where he became known to some as the world's first extreme skier. The segues that led from one chapter of his life to another were often the most unbelievable parts of his entire story. Example: Dag was walking down a flight of stairs in Green Park, just next to Buckingham Palace, when he caught the attention of a casting agent, launching one of the odder chapters in his life. It was 1963, and he had been in London only a few hours with some of his fellow ski instructors, on a break from his job in Scotland, when he flipped upside down and executed a gymnastic party trick. An agent who happened to be in the park watched from a distance as Dag started walking down a flight of stairs on the palms of his hands. The agent waited until Dag reached the bottom of the stairs and flipped back onto his feet. Then he approached and jokingly asked Dag if he was able to go up the stairs on his hands as well. Dag quickly got back on his hands and started climbing the stairs upside down.

The man asked Dag if he had any representation. Dag had no idea what he was talking about. Then the agent handed Dag his card and told him to come by if he had any interest in being in the movies.

The next day, Dag put on a shirt and a tie and a corduroy jacket and walked into the office of Central Casting Ltd. in Soho. The agency quickly sussed him out, writing down his attributes and flaws. He was tall, blond and muscular. Those were the attributes. But they didn't know what to do about his accent, because it was hard to place. So they marketed him as a versatile extra who could play any number of parts, so long as he didn't talk.

They put him into a photobooth, snapped a few headshots, and before the week was out he was on the set of his first film. He doesn't remember today whether it was *The Yellow Rolls-Royce* (in which he played a butler and a medic), *Fanatic* (a body double for Donald Sutherland) or *The Ipcress File* (a stand-in for Michael Caine), but he knows that before the year was out he had been in 36 films and one TV show and had worked alongside a who's who of 1960s cinema. He played

As a film extra living and working in London during the early 1960s, Dag was cast in multiple films, including *The Ipcress File*, *Fanatic* and *Goldfinger*. (Courtesy of Dag Aabye)

doctors, medics, butlers, soldiers, prisoners, students and more. Not all the films were worth mentioning. He couldn't even remember the plot of *I've Gotta Horse* (a musical comedy starring Billy Fury as himself) or *Gonks Go Beat* (a science fiction fantasy flick considered one of the worst British films ever made). And he wasn't sure that he ever saw *The Secret of Blood Island*, a forgettable war movie set in a prison camp in the South Pacific where British soldiers, one of which was played by him, attempt to hide a female secret agent from their Japanese guards. But he remembered the names of many of the stars he had shared the screen with—Sophia Loren, Omar Sharif, Anthony Quinn, James Coburn, Shirley MacLaine, Ingrid Bergman, Peter Cushing, Christopher Lee, Michael Redgrave and more. Some left a stronger impression than others, but none more than Sean Connery. Dag worked on two Connery films over the course of six months: *Goldfinger*, the third instalment in the Bond franchise, and *The Hill*, a drama set in an army prison in North Africa during the Second World War. Among his least favourite gigs: body double for Donald Sutherland and stand-in for Michael Caine. Sutherland was a star on the rise at the time. Caine was already nearing the top of the industry. Dag said neither of them had much time for the extras hanging around the set.

I wanted to take his word for all of it but it was hard to bridge the disconnect between the solitary mountain man I had come to know and the London-based youth. It was difficult to fact-check any of what he said because none of the roles he claimed to have played were large enough to be credited in any of the films he said he was in.

"Some people struggle to believe me when I tell them I was in the movies," he said. "I don't know why. I never pretend like it was anything special. It was just work. Probably the least exciting work I ever did."

Half the films he had never even seen, though he kept some of the reviews in a scrapbook that he had been lugging around for the last 55 years and which he kept stowed away along with some of his oldest journals under the floor of the bus.

Dag started to cough again. We were in the car, but his lungs were still irritated from all the smoke.

"How do you run in this?" I asked.

It was a few moments before he could clear his throat enough to properly respond. "You can't stand still just because the world is burning," he replied. Then he started coughing again.

"Why don't we just keep driving for a while," I suggested. "See if we can get away from the smoke."

By the end of the day we had put so many kilometres behind us that we were closer to the Pacific Ocean than we were to his bus.

THE SKY HAD turned a darker shade of red as we descended one mountain pass, crossed the Fraser Valley and began ascending another. The fires were far in the distance now, but there was still no escaping the scent of smoke. Dag's lungs were still irritated from it all. He sat in the passenger seat, falling into periodic fits of coughing while I drove into the smoky night toward the coast. We had no destination in mind other than the sea. The sun had already gone down by the time we pulled off the highway and checked into a roadside motel. Dag sat outside the room I had rented for him. He had picked up a case of beer while I checked us in and now he was writing in his journal. Every now and again he looked up from the page to watch as the lights from a transport truck appeared out of the haze.

I sat down next to him and took in the surreal night. I could hear the trucks coming from a long way away but I couldn't see them until they were about 20 metres in front of us. They no sooner passed us by before they disappeared again—enveloped by smoke. I looked at Dag and the 12-pack of beer by his side. It was already half gone.

"It will be nice to get to the Pacific," I said. "Leave this hell behind."

He looked at me, then back at the red lights fading into the fog. "There's a beauty to this," he said.

"In an apocalyptic way, I guess." I looked at him again. Then at the empty beer cans by his feet. "How are your lungs?"

"Fantastic."

I still had questions about the movies he had

been in. "Did you actually aspire to work in film?"

"Never," he said. Then he added: "I'll tell you something about movie stars, Brett. They are no different from anyone else. Some of them have time for people, and some of them don't."

"Almost every story I've ever read about you mentions James Bond," I said. "Why do you think that is?"

He shook his head. "*Goldfinger* was such a brief moment in my life. People see me and the way I live and they can't understand it. Then they hear that I was in a movie they once saw and they think 'Wow, that's so interesting.' It's all make-believe. People just want make-believe. So I tell them: I died five times in that movie."

"Is that normal?"

"For an extra, sure."

"What I don't understand, though," I said, "is why people think you were a stuntman for George Lazenby and Roger Moore."

"People think I skied for Bond in *On Her Majesty's Secret Service*. I wasn't even in that movie. But someone once wrote that I did all the skiing for George Lazenby and then someone else wrote the same thing and it didn't matter that it wasn't true because people already believed it." He pointed to his journal. "It doesn't matter what other people write or think about me," he said. "What matters is what I think of myself. I know who skied for Bond in the later movies. He was a tall German guy. He thought the world of himself. I was never the greatest skier. I was just the skier that the greats didn't want to be seen beside. It's all ego."

"What about *your* ego?" I asked. "Does it not get in your way?"

The question seemed to stump him for a moment. Suddenly he laughed. "Look at me," he said. He grabbed his shirt, which was riddled with holes, and held out his hands so I could look at his fingers, which were clawed and knotted by arthritis. "Do I look like I'm driven by ego?"

"What are you driven by, then?" I asked.

We could already hear another truck coming out of the smoke. It roared past and then faded into the darkness once more. Dag had moved on from my question by the time the truck was gone.

"I'll tell you something about Stein Eriksen," he said. "Stein always made sure that you skied behind him. But he was an example of pure confidence. I got to ski with Stein on a glacier in Norway where he was training instructors. I had just gotten out of the army and was focused on being a ski instructor. Some of the other instructors were making fun of my accent because I sounded like a country kid. And Stein, he put his arm around me and told them that I was his friend. Here was the best skier in the world, putting himself out there to help me. I saw him again years later at a chalet in Vail and he was having breakfast with this old guy. I spotted them and I stopped to say hi to Stein and he remembered me and he told me to sit with them. I sat down and it turns out the other guy was Enzo Ferrari."

"Are you sure it was Ferrari?" I asked. I didn't know much about Enzo Ferrari, but I had heard that the Italian was an extremely idiosyncratic human being who rarely travelled far from his hometown of Modena in northern Italy. He never visited Rome, took an airplane or even got on an elevator. So it seemed implausible that he had crossed the Atlantic for a ski vacation. I showed Dag a photo of Ferrari on my phone. "That's the guy," he insisted. He even knew the name of the restaurant where he met him—Pepi's Restaurant and Bar in the Gasthof Gramshammer. Dag said Ferrari had travelled to Colorado to ski with Eriksen and that he was fascinated by the art of racing on skis. "The science of racing is the same whether you're on skis or on a racetrack," Dag said. It didn't matter who was the fastest going into a turn. It only mattered who was the fastest coming out.

Another truck roared into and out of sight.

Now I was the one who changed the subject. "Why did you stop acting in the end?" I asked.

The answer he gave, coupled with my doubts about his meeting Ferrari, made me concerned. He said the reason he stopped acting was the same reason he ultimately left London. "I got arrested," he said. Then he started into a story that was both incomprehensible and unbelievable.

He said one day he was walking along the street when he ran into a guy selling portable radios. Radios were hot commodities in 1964, so Dag bought one. He was on his way home when two police officers approached him. A truckload of radios had just been stolen and the police were arresting anyone they spotted carrying one. Soon he was on his way to Scotland Yard. He could still remember the number of the cell the police threw him into. For a while, he thought the police were just trying to scare him, but then a guard opened the cell door, called Dag by an Indian name and told him that he was being transferred. The next thing he knew he was in shackles and on his way to Brixton Prison. That's where his story got really weird. He told me you had to be sentenced to eight years or more to go to Brixton Prison. Dag didn't remember exactly how long he was there—"one week at least"—but he remembered some particulars about life inside. He said the inmates were all kept in individual cages and that the food was all meat pies and puddings. "It tasted like there was shit in the pies," he said. He quickly developed serious stomach issues. "I'd never been so constipated," he said. "They couldn't fix me in the infirmary so they took me to the hospital. And I'm getting probed and it's awful, the guards were on the other side of the curtain talking football. I looked around and saw that the doctors had left their masks and coats and caps next to the bed. So I put on a green cap, a mask and a doctor's coat and snuck out of the hospital. And that's how I escaped Brixton Prison."

"Are you making this up?" I asked pointedly.

He swore it was true. "I haven't even told you the craziest part," he said. "I later ran into the guys who had arrested me and I told them what happened. They were so afraid that I was going to tell my story to the newspapers that I got a written apology from the secretary of the Queen of England. I wish I had kept it."

I was convinced he believed everything he was telling me, but it all seemed too far-fetched. I made a mental note to ask him about it again some other time to see if the details changed in the next telling (they didn't). Then I told him I was going to bed. He nodded, opened his eighth beer of the evening and continued watching the trucks fade into and out of the smoke while I retired to my room for the night.

The absurdity of Dag's prison story kept me up. Soon I found myself sitting on my bed with my laptop open trying to fact-check whatever I could from what he had just told me. I reviewed the list of films he said he had been in and was soon downloading several of them. At two in the morning I was still up, fast-forwarding through old films in search of Dag. He wasn't always easy to find, but sure enough, he was in the films, just as he had described—a soldier in *Goldfinger*, a butler in *The Yellow Rolls-Royce*, etc. It was pushing three when I fell asleep with my laptop on my stomach. It was just after seven when I opened my eyes. I pulled the blinds and opened the door. A note rested on the mat outside: "Running. 5:30 a.m."

The sun was up but the air was still so full of smoke I couldn't see the horizon. I packed my bag and went outside with a coffee. The garbage can next to Dag's door was overflowing with beer cans. He had polished off the 12-pack by himself. I was amazed he was still able to drag himself out so early to run.

It was 8 a.m. by the time he found his way back to the motel, after cutting a trail through rolling hills of wild sage. I told him I had spent most of the night looking for him in the old movies while also questioning everything he had ever told me.

"I'm not sure everything you said last night is based in reality," I said.

He squinted at me, and I wondered for a moment if he was disappointed by my lack of faith. Then he asked, "Were you able to find me in any of those movies?"

"Yes," I said.

He nodded. "There's one thing my father taught me when I was a kid," he said. "If you can't prove something, then don't talk about it."

FOURTEEN

THE WORLD'S FIRST EXTREME SKIER

He had this tragic mystery about him. He told me he had been found abandoned on a church step. I didn't know until a week before we got married that he actually had a family.

—TONY AABYE, DAG'S EX-WIFE

We continued west, driving through the day and winding through smoke-filled valleys in search of clean air and a clear sky. We found both in Vancouver—550 kilometres from where we had begun our journey. The smoke was behind us now and the sea breeze was rolling off the Pacific Ocean, cooling us down and airing out our clothes. The Lions Gate Bridge straddled the periphery of our vision as we stood on the shores of Vancouver harbour, looking back the way we came toward a snow-capped mountain concealed by a cloud. We had driven into the city just a few hours earlier and were walking the seawall, hoping for a momentary glimpse of a twin-peaked mountain where Dag made skiing history and where he also nearly killed himself 50 years earlier. I had heard the story before. About how on February 17, 1969, he accidentally triggered an avalanche while attempting a solo run down one of the most treacherous mountains yet to be skied. It was a singularly stupid stunt that earned him a reputation as the first extreme skier.

Dag knew before he climbed out of the chopper that morning that his life was in danger. He had triggered and survived two previous avalanches, once in Chile and once while working on a ski film in Whistler. He was fortunate to escape both with minor injuries. He swore after the second avalanche that he would never risk skiing off-piste when the conditions were ripe for a snow slide. And yet he allowed himself to be dropped off alone at the top of a 1,500-metre virgin peak with cornice cracks and walls of snow just waiting to dislodge from the mountain's crust.

The city of Vancouver glistened in the morning sun in the valley below as the chopper lifted up from the mountainside. The air was cool, the sky clear. There were more than a million people circulating within the bustling city sprawled out beneath him, and he wondered whether any of them were looking up at the Lions peaks and the connecting ridgeline on which he stood. Visible from most of the city, the iconic Lions, namesakes of the BC Lions and the Lions Gate Bridge, were so high that anyone looking in his direction would have needed a telescope to spot him.

Dag lowered his eyes as the helicopter hovered overhead. He was 27 years old and perched on the edge of a 60-degree cliff. He clicked his boots into his bindings, lifted his goggles and cast his eyes over the edges of his skis. He was scared. It wasn't the vertical drop that frightened him so much as the overall condition of the snow beneath his skis. Two feet of powder had fallen the previous day, concealing cracks in the compromised crust that made up the base layer on the mountain. The season had been warm, causing large swaths of snow and ice to break off from the mountains without warning. The sun shone down, slowly melting the snow on his skis.

He pushed himself over the ridge and carved his first turn into the snow. Then he jump-turned in the other direction. With every turn he dislodged clumps of snow from the mountain and sent them tumbling fast as he settled into a rhythm, careful not to gather too much speed and accidentally launch himself into a freefall. He was conscious of the overall aesthetic that his turns were leaving on the mountainside. He was putting on a show, not for the oblivious mass below but for the photographer circling overhead in the helicopter.

Deni Eagland, a photographer with the *Vancouver Sun*, kept his camera's lens focused on Dag from inside the chopper, tracking the line Dag was cutting between the boulders and cliffs as he navigated his way down terrain that had never been navigated by anyone. Dag had completed only four turns and Eagland hadn't yet filled his first roll of film when he saw something that Dag could not—a massive crack cutting across the mountainside. The crack stretched about 100 metres wide. There was no way to warn Dag of the impending danger. So Eagland just kept shooting.

Dag couldn't hear the mountain rumbling over the pulse of the chopper's blades, nor could he feel the snow beneath him starting to give way. He executed one more turn. He never saw the crevasse forming in the mountain crust right in front of him. The next thing he knew he was airborne, propelled by a moving wall of snow that seemed to punch him in the back of the legs and then carry him up. He had no control.

Press photographer Deni Eagland was circling overhead in a helicopter when he snapped a photo of Dag right as the avalanche began. (Material republished with the express permission of: *Vancouver Sun*, a division of Postmedia Network Inc.)

There was no time to think, either. The only thing that went through his mind was a realization that he was about to die and that there was nothing he could do to save himself. He didn't hear his ski break in half. Soon his gloves, tuque, goggles and skis were all ripped from his body as he was swept up by the avalanche.

Eagland watched as Dag's blue jacket disappeared and reappeared only to disappear again as the snow cloud barrelled down the mountain. The cameraman tried to keep a visual on the stricken skier inside the expanding avalanche, but it was impossible. Dag was out of sight now, and from Eagland's vantage it seemed likely he was dead.

Dag was freefalling along with the avalanche when suddenly he got lucky and slid into a snow well behind a tree. He grabbed on to a few branches as his body tumbled into the well and managed to stop his descent. Dag pressed his body as close to the tree as possible, using it as a natural buffer. The tree's trunk was parting the snow, allowing Dag to watch as the avalanche rumbled past on each side of him. Then everything went quiet. There was no more roar from the avalanche. No more sound from the chopper, either.

It was a dangerous mix of arrogance and naivety that had brought Dag to the top of that mountain. Days earlier he had sat in a Vancouver tavern, looking out at the Lions through a pair of binoculars and listening as Eagland sold him on the concept of a death-defying photo op. Eagland was 13 years into his career as a news photographer and one of the top shooters in the Vancouver mediascape, but he wanted to put himself on the radar of *Sports Illustrated* and *TIME* magazines. What he needed was an action shot like none anyone had ever seen before. That's where Dag came in.

By the winter of 1969, Dag was renowned as one of the wildest skiers on the planet. He had arrived in the Canadian Rockies three years earlier and quickly become the first star of the newly opened Whistler ski resort. There, he built a reputation as a freestyle skier at a time when there wasn't really such a thing as freestyle skiing. His ascent on the slopes coincided with skiing's exploding popularity. Nearly half of the world's estimated 5,500 ski areas were built in the 1960s. Skiing was North America's fastest-growing sport that decade. Part of its allure was that it was one of the few sports where celebrities and members of high society could be found on the same mountain as middle-class tourists and ski bums. Brigitte Bardot, Audrey Hepburn, Grace Kelly, Hugh Hefner, Paul Newman, Robert Redford, Frank Sinatra, Hunter S. Thompson,

Natalie Wood, the Beatles and Jackie Kennedy—they all played a part in the era's ski boom.

The sport's popularity had grown quickly after the 1952 Olympics. Stein Eriksen, the darling of those Olympics and the sport's first global superstar, was a big part of its early traction. Eriksen relocated to America shortly after the Olympics and began teaching celebrities and everyday Americans how to carve up the slopes at burgeoning resorts in Idaho, Michigan, Vermont, California and Utah before attaching himself to Snowmass and Aspen in Colorado. Soon other ski hills began recruiting famed European skiers to help build their hills' reputations as world-class ski destinations. Europe's best skiers flocked to resorts across North America, taking on jobs as ski pros and helping to drive up ticket sales from the Laurentians in Quebec to the Sierra Nevada in California. As the sport grew, the chance for fame and recognition did too, especially after directors like Warren Miller began shooting and screening ski films all across the continent.

Skiing in North America, from the western Rockies to the Appalachian/Adirondack/Laurentian mountains in the east, evolved slowly after being imported by Sondre Norheim, the Norwegian ski maker and father of the Telemark design, who immigrated to Minnesota in 1884 before settling in North Dakota, where he is said to have always kept a pair of skis by his door. By the mid-1960s, advances in chairlift technology were revolutionizing the ski business and granting visionary developers the means to extract inordinate wealth from ski hills. Formerly small winter tourist towns were transformed into full-on ski resorts whose economies relied on luring middle-class families out of the cities and into their villages to sleep, sup and explore the nearby slopes.

As postwar prosperity spread across North America and western Europe, alpine skiing went from being an elite pastime that few could afford to something that catered to the upper-middle class. Like the sportscar boom of the same era, skiing came to embody the democratization of luxury. Hunter S. Thompson captured the phenomenon in *The Great Shark Hunt* when he wrote, "Skiing is no longer an esoteric sport for the idle rich, but a fantastically popular new winter status-game for anyone who can afford $500 for equipment." Thompson, who had moved from San Francisco to a small hamlet just outside Aspen at the height of the "ski boom," credited the advent of snow-making machines and the proliferation of ski towns for the boom: "The Midwest is dotted with icy 'week-night' slalom hills lit up like the miniature golf courses of the Eisenhower age. The origins of the ski boom were based entirely on economics and the appeal of the sport itself . . . no freaky hypes or shoestring promotion campaigns . . . the Money Boom of the 1960s produced a sassy middle class with time on its hands, and suddenly there was a mushrooming demand for things like golf clubs, motorboats and skis."

But by the late '60s the sport was democratizing more than just luxury. It had begun to democratize thrills as well. While resort owners worked to re-engineer slopes with dynamite and backhoes to safeguard against avalanches and other threats to their clientele, a new breed of skier was beginning to emerge, eager to escape the increasingly manicured nature of the sport. They were powder junkies who preferred skiing on terrain that no other human had ever skied before. Like the era's mountaineers who fixated on the notion of first ascents, this assorted mix of daredevils fixated on first descents.

DENI EAGLAND HELD on for his life as the helicopter twisted in mid-air in a violent manoeuvre. The photographer and the pilot were both trying desperately to regain a visual on Dag's position as the snow cloud from the avalanche carried on down the mountainside. But there was no sign of Dag anywhere.

Down on the mountain, Dag was still in shock at just how close he had come to getting propelled to his death. He was still catching his breath in the tree well that had halted his descent. He stared up into the sky, exhausted, and grateful to be alive.

Dag and I had spoken of the avalanche countless times over the years, and every time he recounted the incident the journalist within me was left craving more from the story. There was no deep revelation that made it all worthwhile. No lesson learned, no change of course. Dag insisted he hadn't been trying to set some obscure record or carve his way into history by becoming the first person to ski the Lions. The story of the avalanche was no more than a near-death stunt that happened to put him around the top of the ski world for a time. I shared this view with Dag as we stood on the harbour wall looking up toward the Lions.

"Maybe some stories don't have a deeper meaning," he replied.

I knew he was right, but I still wanted more.

"Here's the truth about what I did," he said. "I was stupid and I got away with it."

I asked him if he remembered what had gone through his mind as he sat on the snow after the avalanche, waiting for the helicopter to come and rescue him. He said he had thought of his family back home in Sigdal. For the five years leading up to the incident he had been content to never see any of them again. He hadn't sent a single letter to Georg and Helga. It wasn't that he despised the people who had raised him, but he knew that if they knew where he was they would pressure him to return to the farm to become the farmer son they had adopted him to be. So he kept his distance, first heading to Scotland, then London and La Parva, Chile, crossing the South Atlantic on a month-long journey on board a merchant ship. Once there, he spent four months teaching the upper crust of Chilean society how to ski on a jagged Andean peak that rose high above the city of Santiago.

It was in Chile that he began to forge his reputation as the father of freeride. He spent most of his skiing time off-piste in the Andes, preferring the natural, untouched terrain where he could ski without rules to the groomed terrain where he taught everyone else how to ski. Often when he veered off-piste he was venturing where no one else had ever skied, and with every first descent he carved a new image for himself, completely detached from the world into which he had been born.

When the Andean snow began to melt in the fall of 1965, he packed his rucksack, climbed aboard another merchant ship and steamed back to Europe. He had received an offer to teach at a resort in the Austrian Alps. But he never made it to the Alps that winter because there was a letter waiting for him as soon as he arrived in Europe. A massive ski resort had just opened in British Columbia, and the owners wanted Dag to be its resident pro.

Long before it was ever surveyed by the Hudson's Bay Company in 1858, the peak that would ultimately attract Dag to Canada was called Cwítima/Kacwítima by the Lil'wat People and S<u>k</u>wi<u>k</u>w by the Squamish People. Then the surveyors named it London Mountain. But the anglers and hunters who frequented the area had a different name for it. They called it Whistler, because of the high-pitched sound made by the marmots that lived in the rocks that surrounded its base.

By 1960, Franz Wilhelmsen, a Norwegian industrialist based in Vancouver, was determined to develop the mountain into the biggest ski resort on the continent. Born in Trondheim, Norway, in 1918, Wilhelmsen had relocated to Canada shortly after the start of the Second World War. He married one of the heirs of the Seagram family and, together with his wife, wanted to create for Canada a rival to California's Squaw Valley, which had hosted the 1960 Winter Olympics.

Before Whistler's inaugural 1965/66 ski season, Wilhelmsen hired Ornulf Johnsen, a Stein

Eriksen acolyte, to set up the resort's first ski school. Johnsen took one look at Wilhelmsen's creation and said: "A mountain this big needs a big skier."

"Who do you have in mind?" Wilhelmsen asked.

Dag was on a steamship in the middle of the South Atlantic when Johnsen started looking for him. The letter awaiting Dag when he got off the ship in Europe was from Johnsen, and it was accompanied by a one-way ticket to Vancouver. By New Year's Day, Dag was sitting in the passenger seat of a Volkswagen Westfalia driving up a long and winding gravel highway from Vancouver to Whistler.

Johnsen had first met Dag a few years earlier, at Geilo, one of Norway's biggest ski resorts. "I was reading in the lodge and there was this guy outside who built himself a ski jump in the middle of the hill and he kept trying to do a swan-dive-to-front-flip. But he kept landing on his head. I watched him over and over and over again, then suddenly he landed one and then another. That was my introduction to Dag.

"I skied pretty much everywhere, but I never saw anyone who could ski like Dag," Johnsen said. "He was the most athletic person I ever met. He had an elegance and style, even when he was coming over a cliff, that set him apart. He didn't look like he was making any effort. It's hard to pinpoint, but he was just in a different class. He was even better in deeper snow."

When Johnsen brought Dag to Whistler he hoped the acrobatic young skier could wow both the instructors and the clientele flocking to the resort. Johnsen's boss, Wilhelmsen, still harboured grand aspirations that the ski hill could compete in an Olympic bid, but they both knew that Whistler would struggle to outshine bids from more established resorts in Lake Placid, Salt Lake City, Grenoble and Banff. Every little bit of publicity helped. That's where Dag came in. He would routinely trek out of bounds and explore parts of the mountain that no one else would dare ski and which wouldn't be developed for decades. Before Dag arrived no one had tried to strap their skis to their back and make the half-day climb from the top of the nearest lift to the actual peak of the mountain in order to ski the Whistler Bowl. Dag rose early one morning, did the climb by himself and then nailed the descent. Others woke up and looked in amazement at his tracks in the snow.

By the end of Whistler's inaugural season, Dag had been recruited to ski in a number of ski films that would take him to mountains in North and South America. While on location in Bariloche, Argentina, shooting a Warren Miller–

type film, Dag looked on from a mountainside as the military chopper that had been ferrying him around the Andean peaks lost altitude and crashed in a ball of flames. Four people died in that accident. Dag watched as only the pilots climbed out of the wreckage. Fifty years later he still struggled to talk about it. After the accident he returned to Vancouver, and from there got on a train to El Paso before crossing into Mexico and carrying on by another train to Mexico City, and then onward by bus all the way to Santiago, where he had skied the previous summer. He spent the summer of '67 once again teaching on the outskirts of Santiago. He rarely spoke of the woman he got pregnant that summer, and when he did, he never spoke her name. He said they weren't together for long before he left and when he last saw her he had no idea that she was pregnant.

It was mid-autumn when he jumped on a plane back to Canada. Then he got an offer to teach skiing at the Playboy Club resort in Lake Geneva, Wisconsin. He quit that job after just a few weeks and hitchhiked his way to Colorado. He didn't even have a shirt by the time he arrived in Aspen. He walked into town in a pair of shorts with nothing but a backpack and a stray dog that had been accompanying him since somewhere between Illinois and Nebraska. There he fell in with Stein

Eriksen's entourage, who helped to get him kitted out for the upcoming ski season. But he never felt comfortable with the degree of celebrity afforded to him and others in Aspen or in nearby Vail. He spent only a few weeks of the 1967/68 ski season dividing his time between the two resorts before skipping town. By the winter of 1969 he was back in Vancouver, sleeping on the floor of a friend's apartment on Granville Island. That's when Deni Eagland reached out with the proposal to ski the Lions. Heli-skiing was just starting to take off, and Dag knew that if he was going to maintain his place as one of the pre-eminent freestyle skiers he would have to get back into a chopper. And so he did.

Two days later the front page of the *Vancouver Sun* led with an aerial shot taken by Eagland at almost the exact moment that the avalanche began. The caption read: "Avalanche breaks loose from precipitous slope as daredevil adventurer Dag Aabye skis for his life."

Shortly thereafter a US ski magazine called it the most idiotic ski stunt pulled that year. Olympic ski champion Nancy Greene would remember it years later when she said: "You could call Dag the first extreme skier." The moniker stuck.

In the months that followed the avalanche, Dag sent a letter to his parents in Sigdal along with the front page of the *Sun*. "I thought maybe they would be proud, but they weren't proud," he recalled. His mother sent him a simple reply asking if he was suicidal. "You don't care about your parents," she wrote. "You don't care about anyone." It was a long time before he reached out to them again.

Fifty years after the avalanche, Dag reflected on how fortunate he was to have survived. "If that tree hadn't been there," he said, "I wouldn't be here."

"You're lucky you didn't die," I said.

He nodded. Then he repeated a quote he had read years before, though he had long ago forgotten its author. "Solitary trees, if they grow at all, they grow strong."

FIFTEEN

ATONEMENT

We are eternity's hostage. Captives of time.
—BORIS PASTERNAK, QUOTED IN DAG'S JOURNALS

I stood inside Dag's bus for the first time, confronted by the full reality of his existence. A bed of coals glowed in the stove near the middle of the bus. I stepped around sleeping bags, piles of newspapers, a plastic margarine tub, some cutlery and innumerable stacks of books as I made my way toward the back, where Dag had built his bed. Two framed photographs hung on a makeshift wall next to his bed. The first was of a boy and girl, twins smiling at each other. The other was of an arctic wolf, standing alone on the tundra. The first photo was taken by Dag around

1978, when he was a family man living in a suburban home with his wife and three children. He had shot the photo of his youngest children with a camera he purchased while working, for a brief time, as a freelance press photographer while recovering from a logging injury. The portrait of the wolf was a gift from an old friend. On dark, lonely nights, Dag lay on his bed with his headlamp on and looked at the portraits on the wall. They had hung there for 20 years, accumulating dust and grime, cobwebs and mould.

It was early autumn 2018 and we were three years into our friendship when Dag finally invited me inside the bus. I had only seen the bus once before, from a distance. It had looked idyllic and quaint, like something out of a fairy tale—concealed in the shadow of cedars, smoke billowing from its chimney. Now that I was inside, the fairy-tale image was quickly replaced by one of squalor. He kept the archives of his life inside the bus. His journals, photo albums and old correspondence lined its walls and were stacked on the floor, as well as on the driver's seat and under the wooden plank that served as his bed frame. He wasn't a hoarder, but the bus was packed with sentimental keepsakes and overrun by dirt and garbage.

For 20 years, the bus had been located on the edge of a privately owned chunk of untamed forest. It could not be seen from any road, nor by satellite. It had been dragged into its position up a steep incline to a flat spot in the forest, where it was wedged between mature wild cedars, their boughs slowly growing over the bus, concealing it from sight. Since-lost friends and sympathetic acquaintances from an untenable period of Dag's life, when he was a 60-year-old itinerant in Silver Star village, had dragged the bus to this very spot so that he might live in peace and avoid conflict with those who had begun to view him as a burden to society.

Dag always said he enjoyed the seclusion of the forest, but it wasn't always clear how secure he felt inside the bus. He had told me that he once returned to the bus to find it riddled by shotgun fire. Another time he told me he believed someone might light it on fire. Then one day he called me to tell me that someone had broken into his bus while he was out for a run. "I wanted you to know," Dag said, "so there's a record in case anything happens."

I asked whether he felt he was in danger.

He didn't answer right away but eventually said no.

It was all a bit unnerving. "Do you want me to help get you out of there?" I asked.

I was unsure what I could do to help. I lived 4,000 kilometres away in downtown Toronto. I offered to let one of his children know what was going on, but he told me not to. He said he didn't want to be a bother to any of them. They were all far away from him anyway.

I didn't probe any further. Instead I booked a flight and went out to see him a month later. By then he didn't seem to be in any danger, though he did appear to be struggling more with the difficulties of his chosen way of life. The wear and tear on his body was showing, and though he was still extraordinarily fit for a 78-year-old man, his injuries were changing the way he interacted with his surroundings. His right arm was becoming increasingly useless to him, but he compensated by using his left arm for just about everything.

I had often wondered how he managed to live the way he did without proper medical care for any of his ailments. He had lost several teeth in a logging accident years earlier but hadn't been to a dentist in nearly three decades, and several of the teeth he had left were broken. He said his teeth served him well enough, and when they didn't he just used his hands to break his food apart. His hands, though, were slowly gnarling with arthritis. His shoulder was still dislocated. All aspects of his life were getting increasingly complicated. He had no toilet or running water. He bathed out of a pot that he

Dag's bus hadn't moved in 20 years. It had been dragged up a hillside and parked next to wild cedars. He considered the bus his lair and rarely let anyone visit. (Courtesy of the author)

would heat on the stove. Over the years he had dug countless latrines in the surrounding forest (he said he averaged three bowel movements a week) and tended to urinate off the side of his trails. He rarely used an actual toilet, though he did sometimes go into public washrooms when he was in town, taking advantage of soap dispensers to wash his hands.

He had fallen several times in the years I had known him, and though he didn't say so, it became clear to me that by the summer of 2018 he was finding it increasingly difficult to keep things sanitary inside the bus. I offered to help him remove some garbage. He thought about it for a while, then agreed, and soon I was standing inside the bus for the first time, with a growing understanding of what it truly meant to live as he did.

He kept the inside of the bus in perpetual darkness. He said this was to preserve warmth in the winter and to keep it cool in the summer, but it made it feel like a cavernous lair. Not a single shred of light could find its way inside. He had covered every window with either cardboard or drapes. I turned on the flashlight on my phone so that I could see and was immediately overwhelmed by the piles of books that spilled out from the walls and spread onto the floor. There must have been hundreds of them. He said he had read every word of every book he had ever brought into the bus. The wood stove was still warm and the whole place smelled like a bonfire. I ran my hand over the top of the stove, instantly transporting a layer of soot to my palm. Dag stood in front of me, checking a line of socks that hung from a string above the stove. They were almost dry. There wasn't much room to manoeuvre with the two of us inside, even though it was a full-length school bus. He had blankets and sleeping bags spread out on the floor, creating a layer of insulation that kept the heat and the cold from finding their way into his lair.

Amid the mess were several framed portraits of his children and posters for old ski films. Then there were the journals—hundreds of them. They were piled several feet high and spread across the cushions of a couch and on shelves that he had built into the walls.

I shone my light onto one of the piles. "I knew you had a lot of journals in here, but I didn't know there would be this many," I said.

He reached for the nearest stack, grabbed a couple of journals off the top and handed them to me. "Here," he said. "You can have these."

I was surprised by the gesture. "Are you sure?" I asked.

"If you can make sense of them, then maybe you can make sense of me," he said.

He went to a bench near the front of the bus that had a stainless-steel pot filled with water. He splashed some water on his face, then stepped back outside. For a moment I stood alone inside the bus feeling both privileged and guilty to have been let so deep inside his world. I shone my flashlight around the bus again, examining the pictures and the books that he had chosen to surround himself with. Beneath the mould, soot, grease and dust were sentimental reminders that he had once been a family man, but now he was alone and living in what many might consider abject poverty.

I stepped out of the bus to rejoin Dag. He was standing on a nearby trail, clearing a few branches that had fallen to the ground in a heavy wind. I watched for a moment as he struggled to lift a branch from his path. It wouldn't budge. He looked at it, then up at the tree it had fallen from, and nodded to himself.

He saw me and walked back in my direction. He had piled bags of garbage beside the bus. He picked up a stick, ran it through the bags, then raised them onto his shoulder and asked if I could grab the others that he could not carry. I did so, and together we walked with loads of trash through the forest and down to my car. We filled the trunk, then returned for more and filled the back seat too. Then we climbed inside and began driving away.

I LEFT AT the end of that trip with a fuller appreciation for how Dag lived. But I still didn't know how he had ended up in a bus surrounded by artifacts from a life he had already lost. So I turned to the one person who would be able to fill in some of the blanks: Dag's ex-wife.

When Tony Aabye learned that I was a journalist who had befriended her former husband, she was immediately curious whether I had solved the mystery at the core of his existence. "Have you found out where he came from?" she asked.

"I always wondered if he would ever find out the truth, but I figured by this point in his life it would never happen."

The last time Tony had laid eyes on her former husband, he was sitting at a bar drinking Kokanee and staring blankly at her face, unable to place her in the confines of his memory.

For more than 20 years she had been his wife. Nearly as many years had passed since their breakup. For the first few years after they split, he would sometimes reappear at the home they had once shared in the Okanagan, step inside and proceed to talk with her as if nothing between them was broken. It had taken Tony seven years to divorce Dag and sever their lives entirely. Then she moved 1,300 kilometres east to Saskatchewan to start a new life.

After about 15 years without seeing him, she returned to Vernon to visit her sister. She was midway through her lunch at a restaurant when a familiar figure walked in from the forest and sat down at the bar. She recognized Dag immediately, though he no longer looked anything like the man she once loved. His clothes were tattered, his hair matted and his beard fuller than she remembered it. She finished her meal and watched him from a distance. She contemplated just paying her bill and leaving the restaurant without saying hello. But she suspected that once she left, she would never see him again. There was nothing left between them to be said, no feelings to express, but she didn't want to look back years later and regret not having said one final goodbye to the man who had once been the most important person to her. So she walked slowly toward the bar, put her hand next to his and said hello.

He raised his head and looked at her, but had no idea who she was or why she was talking to him.

She watched as he struggled to place her face. She wasn't hurt that he didn't recognize her, though she was surprised. Finally, she spoke. "I don't know if you know me anymore," she said, "but I'm your ex-wife."

He squinted, then nodded. "Oh yeah," he said.

For a moment that was all he said. Then they spoke for a while, until Tony told him goodbye and walked out of his life yet again.

She had wondered, over the years that followed, if he ever reflected on the life they once built together. Or the family they had raised or the dreams they had shared. Once upon a time, she had found him to be the easiest person to love. But she also found him to be the hardest person to understand.

She was 19 when she met him. He was 26. She was working as a ski patrol at Mount Seymour, a ski hill just outside Vancouver, where she grew up, when he appeared from out of nowhere in the winter of 1968 after slipping over the US-Canada border in the trunk of a car, without proper documentation, on his way north from Aspen. He quickly joined the mountain's ski school as an instructor, though he spent more time training the other instructors than he did teaching any students. She had never heard of him, until they met one morning at a meeting of all the ski patrols and instructors at the base of the hill. She had arrived late and was being reamed out by their mutual boss when she noticed him smiling at her. "He winked at me and I just about melted," she remembered. "I never, ever thought I would get involved with him. I was this skinny kid and he was—honestly, as far as skiers went, he was famous. That was the first time I ever saw him and, I think, the first time he ever noticed me." She watched as the other ski patrols and instructors gathered around him like he was some sort of ski god. She got to know him first by reputation as a playboy and a mystery.

At first, they were just good friends. Then they became more than that. There was a vulnerability to him that attracted her more than anything he was able to do on skis and which revealed itself to her over time as the two grew closer. She first picked up on it one evening when

By the late 1960s, Dag's reputation as one of the world's most daring skiers had earned him more fame than he craved, especially in Aspen and Vail. (Cliff Fenner, courtesy of the Whistler Museum)

she asked him where he came from and how he wound up in Canada.

"He told me he was found on the step of a church," recalled Tony. She remembered the story vividly and the way he told it: he said he had been abandoned on a church step in the middle of the war and the clergy had taken him in to await adoption and that everyone in his life was dead. "It just seemed so tragic and sad," she said.

They bonded as friends on the ski hill that winter and the next. Then came the avalanche on the Lions.

"People said it was a stupid stunt, but he was smarter than that. Everyone in skiing, everyone, was talking about it. He had pages of articles written about him. Everyone was saying 'Oh my god, did you hear what Dag did?' It was pretty amazing. He should have used it as a stepping stone, to really become *the* only skier that mattered. But he didn't."

She believed that he had been damaged by something before she even met him, but she didn't really know what it was. She guessed it was the helicopter crash he witnessed in South America. "He told me once that all he could hear was screaming," she said. "I think they ran to the crash site to see if they could save anyone. My understanding is that it was awful. It changed him. He never wanted to get on a helicopter again."

They moved in together shortly after the avalanche, and before long she knew she wanted to marry him. She recalled how, after they had lived together for two years, she said to him, "'Look, we're either going to get married or we separate. What do you want here?' He said, 'Oh, you're pressuring me.' I said, 'I love you, I would love to have a family with you.' I went out and when I came back he was gone. All his stuff was gone. I thought that was okay. Then Monday morning came and he was back, saying, 'Let's get married.' He had gone to Whistler to see if he wanted that life instead and then he came back."

It was a week before the wedding when he sat her down, took out a photo album and showed her pictures of Hovlandsmoen, of Georg and Helga and the life he had run away from in Norway. It was the first time he had ever spoken of the farm or of his adoptive parents. Then he opened the letter from Chile and showed her the photo of the son he had never met. He said the boy was five and that he didn't know his name. He didn't share much else of his story. And what he held back, he kept to himself for the rest of their marriage.

SIXTEEN

ALIENATED FROM BIRTH

*We will never be rid of the stigma, not
until we are dead and buried . . . I don't
want to be buried in a grave; I want my
ashes to be scattered to the winds—at least
then I won't be picked on anymore.*

—PAUL HANSEN, NORWEGIAN LEBENSBORN CHILD

Dag never knew for certain the circumstances that led to his birth. He didn't know whether he was a Lebensborn child, the product of an assault or the unwanted result of a short-lived relationship between a German soldier and a Norwegian woman. The absence of certainty shielded him from many of the retributions against *tyskerunger*—German brats. But it did not shield him from the trauma that was borne by the children of the war.

Long after the fall of Berlin, the children who had been left behind by German soldiers in Norway continued to be emotionally scarred by their association with Heinrich Himmler and the mass breeding experiment of the Third Reich. Abandoned, first by their biological parents and then by their adoptive ones, many were institutionalized. Others were deported. Only the lucky ones grew up oblivious of who they were or what they were meant to represent. Many of them developed a deep-rooted sense of shame.

For more than 70 years, Dag thought that perhaps he was one of the Lebensborn, but he was never branded as such publicly. Though many in Sigdal suspected he was one of the children the Nazis left behind, no one could say for certain. Even though he wasn't beaten and harassed like so many Lebensborn children, there were people in his life who wondered if he was emotionally damaged by association.

As Tony told me: "I always felt that the uncertainty over who he was left a big impact on him. But I don't know that he ever understood it that way."

IT MADE SENSE that Dag believed he may have been one of the 12,000 children fathered by German soldiers during the war. Only 8,000 were ever officially registered as children of the Third Reich under the banner of the Lebensborn. Most were adopted by sympathetic families eager to nurture the myth of Aryan superiority. Thousands of the children were branded mentally ill by Ørnulf Ødegård, one of Norway's leading psychiatrists. The designation, though not officially adopted by the state, spread among the public. The mothers didn't have it any easier, being branded mentally unfit by the same psychiatrist.

Soon after the war was over, the Norwegian state drew up plans to deport the children to Germany. But that plan was abandoned after the Norwegian government recognized that if it sent the children to Germany it would be dispatching thousands of toddlers into a humanitarian crisis. Sweden was the next choice. Though only 30 children were ever officially sent to Sweden, countless others were quietly carried over the border to escape reprisals, the most famous being Anni-Frid Lyngstad, one of the lead singers of ABBA, who was born six months after the war ended. Lyngstad's father had been a sergeant in the Wehrmacht who was sent back to Germany before her birth.

In November 1945, six months after the occupation ended, officials reached an agreement that would have relocated 9,000 of Norway's war orphans to Australia. But by late 1946, the plan had been deemed unfeasible, and it was decided the children would have to be raised on Norwegian soil.

As far as Dag knew, he was one of the lucky ones. Having been adopted to Hovlandsmoen, he had escaped the fate that befell those children who were rounded up from orphanages and sent to live in institutions for the mentally ill.

For decades the plight of the Lebensborn children went largely unreported. Then, in the early 2000s, a team of Norwegian historians and sociologists began collecting the stories of survivors. Among the horrifying stories of sexual assault and abuse were numerous accounts of children being regularly beaten simply because of their parentage. One woman told how her adoptive parents tried to "beat the German hell out of [her]" while classmates routinely lashed out at her. She reported that a dentist once intentionally drilled into her jaw to let her feel what it was like to be tortured. When she was 10, a group of villagers got drunk and branded a swastika on her forehead.

Speaking to the BBC in 2007, Bjorn Lengfelder, a Lebensborn child, said, "In the Norwegian population there was a hatred directed at us children. A small brother and sister, five years old, were placed in a pigsty for two nights and two days. Then in the kitchen they were put in a tub and scrubbed down with acid till they had no skin left 'because we have to wash that Nazi smell off you.'"

Most children didn't try to find their biological parents until adulthood, and if they did they often found mothers who were emotionally scarred themselves and fathers who were either dead or refused to acknowledge them. Some of the children, however, never found anyone. Though the Norwegian National Archives maintains a collection of Lebensborn files, documents tracing the lineage of numerous children remain unaccounted for. A 2004 academic study of 1,150 war children found that although 90 percent of them had married at some point, owned houses and had children of their own, they had a much higher rate of suicide and higher rates of divorce, were more likely to suffer from mental health problems and had lower levels of education and income. The researchers concluded that the trauma, instability, and isolation of their childhoods continued to have an impact on them 60 years after the war. Even those who had been raised in seemingly well-adjusted families reported feelings of alienation.

For 25 years, Norwegian authorities have been wrestling with how to make amends to the children who were victimized and alienated because of the blood that ran through their veins. In a New Year's address marking the year 2000, Norway's prime minister issued a short apology to the Lebensborn survivors. Legal proceedings against the government soon followed, and by 2002 the Norwegian parliament ordered the state to compensate surviving children up to about US$32,000. Though Dag suspected he was one of those children, he never applied for compensation from the state. He didn't want any of it either. All he wanted was to know who his mother and his father were.

In February 2019, I travelled west to return Dag's journals and to share with him the details I had managed to piece together about the Lebensborn and where he might find more information about his parents.

I found him running next to a snowbank on a frozen mountain road near the bus. It was late morning, and Dag was running with ski poles in his hands. He used them for stability on snowy mornings. I walked with him back to a firepit near the bus, where we stood and drank coffee as the snow fell on top of us. His knuckles cracked as he unfurled his fingers and warmed them over the embers. He said he had heard on the radio that morning that scientists had discovered evidence Neanderthals were the world's first artists, drawing on cave walls in Spain 65,000 years ago. It was the type of thing he would later spill into his journal as one of the day's many meaningful discoveries. He had been on his feet for most of the morning and had been running off and on since 4:30, when he had laced his boots and stepped through the hanging blanket that served as the inner threshold of his lair. Now that he was stationary he was trying to keep warm.

He threw another dead pine branch on the fire. The needles crackled and popped while the snow continued to fall in thick, fluttering clumps. I told him I had looked up a quote he had shared with me months earlier because I was curious to know its author.

"'Solitary trees, if they grow at all, they grow strong,'" I repeated. "Turns out it was written by Winston Churchill."

"Is that right?" he replied.

"I googled it and that's what came up."

He looked at me, and it occurred to me that he might not know what Google was. Then he put another branch on the fire.

I had found the quote in a letter from the 24-year-old Churchill to his mother. It was from a book he was writing, and was part of a passage about a Nubian leader who had been orphaned as a child only to become a military opponent of the English during their conquest of Sudan between 1896 and 1899. Churchill, who had a troubled relationship with his own father, had copied it for his mother: "Solitary trees, if they grow at all, grow strong: and a boy deprived of a father's care often develops, if he escape the perils of youth, an independence and a vigour of thought which may restore in afterlife the heavy loss of early days." This was much weightier than what Dag had bothered to remember.

Dag was a voracious reader. We spoke often about the things he read, but he read so much that we rarely spoke about one topic for long. My repetition of his tree quote got him talking about a Douglas fir on Vancouver Island he had recently read about. It was 1,000 years old and 20 storeys high and was the only remnant of an old-growth forest. He had never seen the tree, but he had seen enough old-growth trees of its size and species during his years as a logger that he could visualize its corky bark, a foot thick in parts, and could describe the distinctive aroma of its trunk and the earthy scent of moss and lichen growing on its sides. Dag had an adoration for trees that wasn't just rooted in the fact that a tree had saved his life during an avalanche. He had been taught back at Hovlandsmoen to view trees as a familial resource passed down from one generation to the next. He appreciated them for what they contributed to nature. But also for everything they could become once harvested.

In the summer of 1971, he moved to Squamish, a logging town between Whistler and Vancouver. The ski season had ended and he was looking for work. He had never aspired to be a logger, even though the work had been part of his upbringing in Norway. His mother would often send him into the forest with a pouch full of sandwiches for the lumberjacks and the cotters who worked the family's land. He would sit and eat his own lunch and watch as they felled the trees his grandfather had planted. Then he would watch as they strapped the logs to a team of horses and dragged them down to the river. It was rather artisanal in comparison to the industrial-scale logging operations that were working the hills and valleys that surrounded Squamish. He didn't know what he was getting into until he was already well inside the industry, living in camps up and down the Sunshine Coast and periodically getting called over to Vancouver Island and Haida Gwaii to log the lush rainforests that were home to some of the largest trees in the world. At the time, the logging industry was largely unregulated, the industry's effect on the BC coast not fully understood.

He had no idea how many trees he helped drag out of the forest over his 18 years in the industry. "Tens of thousands," he estimated. "Probably more."

He spent most of his career as a hook tender, in charge of a small crew that worked deep in the forest. He rose quickly through the logging ranks, learning his craft as choke setter, attaching cables to downed logs and then running clear before the big yarder machine fired up its engines and lifted and dragged the heavy logs from where they were felled up to the desired extraction point. He was never the man in charge of picking which trees would fall and which would survive. His job was generally to figure out how to get the trees that were cut safely out of the forest. Sometimes, though, he would be called upon to do the job of the high rigger. High riggers were the kings among loggers. They were the guys who climbed the trees to set the lines. Dag would strap on spurs and a harness, grab his ropes and scale the trunks of centuries-old firs, trimming out branches on his way up to put in a back spar. Back on the ground, he would run cables around stumps, lay the rigging, set the tailholds, prep the skidding and run the saws. He was happy doing all of it.

He was in awe of every tree he ever climbed, though he also understood their value. A single

500- to 1,000-year-old fir could have a diameter of more than two metres and be more than 60 metres tall. When converted to lumber a single tree could frame multiple houses.

There wasn't much time for or interest in existential debate among loggers while out in the forest or back in the camps. It was essential for each logger to trust every other member of the crew with his life. "A lot of people who despise logging don't realize that it's one of the most dangerous jobs on the planet," Dag said. "In logging there are countless ways to get yourself killed." He didn't remember how many loggers had died in the camps over his 18 seasons. Some died by getting crushed by logs rolling on top of them; others were killed by the heavy machinery. Some were killed by flying winches or cables, which would explode under duress and cut through the forest with enough force to sever a man in half. "If you heard a long, hard whistle, that meant someone was hurt or dead," Dag said. "You learn to hate the sound of a whistle when it symbolizes death."

Anytime the whistle blew, Dag would begin looking for his friends. Of all the losses he had known in the forest, none affected him more than the death of a young man whose name would come to haunt him later in life—Erik Hansen. Hansen had been walking along the top of a downed trunk, trimming its limbs and preparing it for transport, when another member of the crew dropped a spruce right on top of him and crushed him.

Dag was married through the entirety of his logging career. He had wed Tony on a rainy January day in 1971 in Stanley Park. They said their vows next to the seawall while the Pacific waves crashed against the shore. They signed their wedding papers in a nearby phone booth, then retired to a teahouse for lunch. The first winter of their marriage they spent skiing together on the slopes at Whistler. Dag was still notorious on the mountain; the fame of surviving the avalanche had yet to wear off. "He was the biggest name in skiing," Tony remembered. "It took a while for that to go away."

On warm nights they cruised around Vancouver or Whistler in his Opel GT sportscar. But by the summer of 1972, the Opel was gone and the couple had relocated to a trailer in Squamish. That's where Dag's past and the people and things he had been running away from for more than a decade finally caught up with him.

Remembered Tony: "He would get these letters and he would sit in the corner of the trailer and he would cry while reading them. I would ask him what's wrong, and he would just say, 'I can't even begin to tell you.'"

She never knew that his parents had been searching for him, or how they ultimately found him. Looking back on the entirety of their marriage, she concluded that she never really felt she knew much about Dag. "There was always this part of himself that he didn't like to talk about," she said. "This wall that he put up to keep everyone out."

They had been married five years when she learned she was pregnant. It was 1976, and as Dag and Tony prepared for the birth of their first child, Helga and Georg showed up in Squamish. They had come hoping to build a bridge to their son and to his new family. Thirteen years had passed since he left them in anger, and they had travelled halfway across the world in the hopes of persuading him to relocate with his wife and child to Sigdal so that he might work toward inheriting Hovlandsmoen.

Tony recalled just how little Dag seemed to have in common with his adoptive parents. Helga had arrived bearing antique gold candlesticks as a housewarming gift. But she took one look at the trailer in which Dag and Tony lived and remarked that the cotters and the lumberjacks they employed on the farm lived in better places than their son. The comment upset Tony more than Dag.

Tony recalled how Helga would be both kind

and terrible toward Dag at the same time. It was as if nothing about Dag could satisfy her.

Helga and Georg were still staying with them when Tony went into labour and gave birth to their first daughter. "What I remember is a day later, Helga came in and she squeezed me so hard, that's what I remember—the pain. I yelped. And she said to me, 'I know what it feels like to have a baby.'" Tony didn't know what to make of that. She knew Dag had been adopted.

Days later, Helga and Georg returned to Norway. Tony never met or heard from either of them again.

For several years thereafter, life in the Aabye trailer was quiet and simple. "We were happy," Tony recalled. "We really were. Dag was a good father in those early years. The real issues that brought him down weren't as visible until later."

In 1978, two years after the arrival of their daughter, Tony gave birth to twins, a boy and a girl. There were long stretches of the kids' childhood when Dag would be absent, away in the forest logging. But when he was home he would try to make up for lost time. He and Tony would have races to see who could change the diaper on one of the twins the fastest, and he made dinner for his family of five in the trailer while Tony went back to school to become a nurse. Dag continued to log through the summers and spent the winters working odd jobs at the local ski hills. He helped set up the trail for competitions at Whistler while teaching children to ski at some of the region's smaller resorts—Mount Seymour or Grouse Mountain. Whatever notoriety he had gained on skis in the 1960s had all but worn off by the end of the decade that followed.

"He sacrificed who he had been in order to make the family work," Tony said. When he did finally step back into the sport, he was no longer a star. "By the start of the 1980s the ski world had passed him by." Extreme skiing was still an exploding corner of the sport, but Dag was in his 40s and no longer getting invited by photographers and filmmakers to climb into helicopters and cut tracks down some untouched mountain. He was a working-class father trying to make it in suburbia. By 1981, he and Tony had saved up enough money to move from the trailer park into a house. Life was coming together for Dag and his young family.

Then the phone rang from family back in Norway. Georg was dead.

SEVENTEEN

FORTUNE'S FOOL

*Don't question who you are but
what you can become.*
—DAG'S JOURNALS

In the years that followed Georg's death, the old manor at Hovlandsmoen became lonely and quiet, its many fireplaces having gone cold one by one as Helga retreated from its rooms, confining her movements to the kitchen, her bedroom, the bathroom and a lone sitting room, where she would often read under an oil painting of the boy she once raised. For a time, she welcomed the charity of family, especially that of her nearby sisters, and from Gunhild, her niece, who lived at Skartum, the nearby farm that had been in Helga's family for more than a century. But the longer Helga spent alone in the house, the more embittered, avaricious and paranoid she became. She grew distrustful of her extended family and didn't seem willing to leave the farm to anyone.

Georg had died of cancer in the late summer of 1981, at the age of 78. Helga was 73 at the time and had never lived alone. Months before Georg's death, Gunhild's second-born son, Bjorn Andreas, had travelled to Squamish to visit Dag and to meet his family. Georg had asked the young Bjorn Andreas, who was 21 years Dag's junior, to ask Dag if there was any chance he would ever come home to take over the farm. Bjorn Andreas passed on the message, but Dag had no intention of ever living at Hovlandsmoen again.

As Georg's health began to fail, the old man gave up and set a plan in motion to sell Hovlandsmoen to Bjorn Andreas. But after Georg's death, Helga demanded more money than Bjorn Andreas could afford, and the deal went nowhere. Despite her own failing health, Helga managed the farm herself, hiring workers to plough the fields, sow the earth and harvest the trees. But by the spring of 1990, she was 82 years old and miserable. She had isolated herself in her house, choosing to live among the many antiques that

Dag had a strained relationship with his adoptive mother, Helga. She struggled to accept him for who he was and hoped he would someday take over Hovlandsmoen. (Courtesy of Dag Aabye)

she had accumulated. As she neared the end of her life, she wrote more and more to Dag, but her letters were often written in anger and dismay. She had long felt abandoned by her only son and never forgave him for walking away from all that she wanted to leave him. She tried to reason with him, to remind him that although he had been adopted he was her son, and that she hoped he would return to the Aabye family home to fulfill his purpose. But the more she pushed, the more distant he became.

Dag returned to Norway only twice over the last 20 years of Helga's life. The first time was in 1981, after Georg's death. He brought his eldest daughter with him on that trip and wanted to ask Helga for more information about his own parentage, but he shied away from posing the question when it became clear that she resented him for not being nearer while Georg was sick. With his daughter at his side, Dag navigated the family relations, reacquainting himself with cousins he hadn't seen in two decades, and met an entire generation of extended family born in the years since he had run away.

Seven more years passed before he returned, in September 1988. Helga was 80 and Dag was himself a man of 47. This time he travelled back to the farm with his youngest son, Hans, who was nine years old and eager to see the place where his father had grown up. Dag had come to make peace with the only mother he had ever known.

For the first few days things seemed to be going well. Helga treated her grandson as if he were her own son, teaching him about the family's history. Then one night, everything changed. Hans never knew what happened between Helga and his father. All he remembered was being awoken in the middle of the night by his father telling him that it was time to go. Then he heard Helga pounding on his bedroom door in the dark, screaming at Dag not to leave.

"She was banging on the door," Hans remembered. "I started screaming. He told me we had to jump out the window and that's what we did. We jumped out the window."

Dag was carrying Hans in his arms by the time they reached Gunhild's home, five kilometres away.

"I don't know what happened between them that night," Gunhild said, "but after that Helga told him that when she died there would be nothing left for him here. No money, nothing."

Dag told Helga that he had never wanted any of her money anyway. The two never reconciled. She put Hovlandsmoen on the market.

The farm attracted media attention beyond the valley because of its value and historical significance. Helga managed to negotiate that she could continue living in the manor, but she sold the farmland and forest to a developer who jumped at the rare opportunity to buy one of Norway's older and more storied properties. Soon she was watching from her window while tree after tree that Georg had planted for Dag's benefit fell. She immediately regretted selling the land and quickly found herself in conflict with the developer. She told him he had no right to cut down the trees, and when he told her to get off his land, she began begging her extended family to help her reverse the sale. The question of who would save her triggered a crisis of inheritance that sucked in multiple branches of her family. The only one who seemed to escape the crisis was Dag, even though he was the person who could most easily have solved it in the first place.

As tensions with the new owner mounted, Helga became increasingly fearful and desperate. Her only salvation lay in the ancient *odelsrett*. By law, even if the property was sold to non-family, family members had the right to reclaim it at the price paid. Given that Dag had no interest in the estate, the rights to the land fell to Helga's eldest nephew, Carl. It took more than a year to sort through the land claims in court. All the while, Helga remained holed up in the manor, watching as the developer and his men felled tree after tree.

By Easter 1990, the farm was safely in Carl's hands, but the ordeal had left Helga emotionally and physically exhausted. Then she suffered a stroke. She departed the old house at Hovlandsmoen in an ambulance and never returned. She lived out the last four months of her life in a long-term care facility. She was nearing the end when she requested that someone reach out to her only son. All she wanted was to see him one last time.

Dag knew Helga was sick but delayed going to see her until he was told there was no more time to waste. He threw some clothes in his old canvas rucksack, drove to Vancouver and took a series of flights back to Norway. He arrived in Sigdal just in time for one final conversation with Helga before she died. He remembered nothing of that conversation other than a single comment. "Your hair is so long," she said. Then she was gone.

FOR THE FIRST time since his childhood, Dag was alone at Hovlandsmoen, wandering through its still rooms. He walked into the dining room, where he used to sit quietly while his parents entertained guests. He went into the living room, which was still filled with expensive antiques, and then into the study, which was lined with custom bookcases holding first editions of age-old texts Helga had collected throughout her life. Dag was eyeing the titles on some of the spines when he noticed that resting atop the bookshelves were the two candle holders Helga and Georg had tried to gift him when they visited him in Canada. The candle holders rested next to a large silver punch bowl under an old oil painting of Dag. Dag couldn't remember sitting for the portrait four decades earlier. He stared at the boy in the painting: aged no more than five, dressed in a collared shirt and vest, with one hand resting on his knee. There was little he recognized of himself in the portrait.

Then he made for the old staircase at the centre of the house. The steps creaked as he climbed toward his childhood bedroom, the one he had escaped from through the window just two years earlier. Then he went back downstairs and out the door. He still wasn't comfortable in the house.

The day after Helga died, the search began for her will. No one knew where to find it or what would be in it, least of all Dag, who understood that he had been cut out of any inheritance. He hadn't come back wanting, or expecting, anything. But as the days turned into weeks, it became clear that Helga had not left a will, and as such, by law everything she had owned was left to Dag. It took a long time for Dag to process this. He didn't know what to make of his newfound wealth. He knew even less what to make of the woman who had left it to him. Then one day shortly after the funeral, Carl came by to inform him that when Helga sold the farm to the developer, she had severed 40 acres of forest and his old cabin from the rest of the farm. It too now belonged to Dag.

"She saved you your cabin," Carl told him.

Dag hadn't been to the log cabin since the early 1960s. Helga had kept it for him in case he ever returned. Everything inside was right where he had left it. His old record player still sat on a table next to the fireplace. The old carpet he used to lie on and listen to music was still there, as was the bed he had made for himself in the small loft space above the kitchen. Even the magazines he read as a teenager were still there, resting by the fireplace along with some of his old letters.

NEWS SPREAD QUICKLY through the valley that Helga had died without a will. The fate of her estate was fodder for gossip. The Aabyes had been wealthier than many in the valley, and it didn't take long for rumours to begin to swirl as to exactly how much Dag had inherited. The revenue from the sale of the farm alone had added several hundred thousand dollars to Helga's estate. But Helga and Georg had a lot of savings already.

Some said Helga had left hundreds of thousands of dollars in a paint can somewhere in the house. Others questioned whether Dag had a right to any of the assets at Hovlandsmoen, given that the land had already been sold to another branch of the family. And there were those who wondered what would become of the antiques that were in every room, some of which were as old as the farm.

Dag was still trying to make sense of what he had been left when his cousin Gunhild handed him a piece of paper with a phone number on it. Gunhild had been one of his closest friends as a child, having grown up on Skartum. She and Dag spent countless hours together as children, exploring the forests on the family estates. But she had always wondered where Dag came from. She heard rumours over the years that his biological father was German, but neither Helga nor Georg nor her own parents had ever spoken to her about it.

She told Dag there was an office in Oslo that held records of children adopted during the occupation. The Germans kept detailed reports on each of the Lebensborn children, and though some of the paperwork had been lost at the end of the war, much of it had survived. She told him that his best chance of finding answers to his questions was to call the number she had just handed him.

Dag folded the paper and put it in his pocket. He was 50 years old and no longer even sure what he wanted to know. He put off calling for a few days and then picked up a phone and started dialing. He doesn't remember how long he was on the phone or who he spoke to or whether it took more than one call, but at some point he found himself speaking to someone who told Dag that he had been born in Oslo and was baptized in an old church near an orphanage in the city's east end. Dag hung up and phoned the church. Soon he was speaking with a parish secretary, who proceeded to dig through a 50-year-old church register to find scraps of information Dag had been looking for his entire life.

Days later he received a letter from the church. It said that his biological parents had named him Erik and that his last name was Hansen. Dag's mind immediately transported him back to the forests north of Squamish. He had known another Erik Hansen. He could still remember the horrible way he died.

Dag carried on reading the letter, which said that according to the church scrolls, his mother's name was Heda Hansen. She was unmarried at the time of Dag's birth. The church couldn't find any information about his father. There was a name in the church book, but there was no way to say for certain whether the name was even real. The letter said that sometimes during the war, the father gave a false name to cover up the fact that he was German.

The letter finished by advising Dag that he might find more information through another office, one that had been set up to assist Norway's war orphans in locating information about their parents. Soon Dag was on the phone again. He learned that, in the months before and after his birth, his mother had been seen in the company of a German U-boat officer, until one day the U-boat steamed out of port and the officer was never seen again. No one had seen his mother since the war ended, but it was believed she had fled to Sweden, where she later died in a car accident.

Then Dag was given one final piece of information: a phone number for someone believed to be from Heda Hansen's family. Dag jotted down the number and worked up the courage to call. He was nervous as the phone began to ring. His birth mother had always been just a shadow in his head, a woman without a face. Without a story. Now that he knew her name he wanted to know more. But above all else, he wanted a photo. Something he could hold on to and study.

A man picked up on the other end. He may

well have been Dag's brother, for all Dag knew. Dag had many questions, but he never got answers to any of them.

"They didn't want anything to do with me," Dag later recalled. "I told them who I was and they just said, 'Are you kidding?' Then they hung up."

He never tried to call again, and as time passed and his life fell apart, he lost the phone number.

DAG STUCK AROUND Sigdal for a few more weeks. Back at Hovlandsmoen he continued to struggle with his newfound wealth. He suddenly had more money than he knew what to do with. He felt uncomfortable inside the house, so he spent the days outside wandering the farm and the forest, and when night fell he would visit one of the many friends and relatives he had in the valley.

One day he went to the post office and found an anonymous letter waiting for him. It had been mailed from a neighbouring valley. It advised him to leave the country with the money he had inherited. Dag read the letter several times. He had no idea who sent it or why. He thought of his family back home, his three children and Tony. It had been a long time since he had seen them. Then he thought of Bjorn Andreas, Gunhild's son, to whom Georg had wanted to leave the farm shortly before his death 10 years earlier.

And he thought of Carl, who had fought to get the farm back in the family after Helga sold it out of spite. Dag wanted to make good by both of them. The next day he sought out Bjorn Andreas and handed him a chunk of the proceeds from Helga's estate. Then he went to visit Carl. "The house is yours," Dag told him. "The only thing I ask is that you keep it as it is. Keep it as she left it."

Then he left for the airport.

EIGHTEEN

DESCENSION

It's the duty of the present to convey the voices of the past to the ears of the future.
—ANONYMOUS QUOTE IN DAG'S JOURNALS

Dag's youngest daughter remembers the day her mother cleaved Dag from her life. It was the morning of his 53rd birthday. His daughter walked into the kitchen and found him sitting at the table, staring at a pile of papers scattered in front of him.

"Happy birthday, Dad!" she said.

He didn't respond.

He always had a way of being absent even when he was present, but she had never seen him look so lost inside his own head. She leaned over the table. "What's this?" she asked.

The divorce papers had been served to Dag by a lawyer earlier that morning. Years later, Tony gave me various reasons for the breakdown of their marriage, including alcoholism and the belief that Dag had squandered or given away an indeterminate amount of money and was on track to drive the entire family into poverty.

Three years had passed since Helga's death. Dag had returned to Canada with some oil paintings, a pair of antique skis and more money than he had earned in his entire life. But by the spring of 1994, the money was all but gone, Dag was out of work and, according to Tony, he was drinking excessively and no longer functioning as a husband or a father. He would spend long nights alone at the bar, pulling out wads of money and handing it to strangers. He treated his inheritance as if it were dead skin, something to shed from his person. Tony recalled him drifting away from his family physically, emotionally and financially.

Looking back on that period in his life, Dag's son, Hans, explained: "As soon as we inherited that money, that's when the tightness severed. He didn't want any of it, and he just started giving it away. If he could, he would give everything to you. Only he knows how much has been taken from him."

By the time Tony filed for divorce, the money was gone, and Dag was paying off his bar tabs with the antique paintings he had brought back from Norway.

No one in his family or his circle of friends knew what was wrong with him or how to help. Tony recalled how difficult it was to watch him give so much of his inheritance away. She said that before Helga's death, Dag had been close with each of his children. "He was a great father," she said. "He would feed them in the middle of the night when they were babies. Some days he was so tired. He would work 12 hours logging, then he would come back and he would have quality time with the kids." When he wasn't away logging, he would throw the kids on the back bench of his red Firebird, drive Tony to work and then head to the ocean and take the kids for a long hike. "He was incredibly good with them when they were young," Tony said. "He would come home from the bush exhausted and absolutely filthy. He would have a bath, have his dinner and then he would read to the kids. Those were the best days of my life. His life really had a purpose." After Helga died, things changed. To Tony, it seemed as though Dag didn't really care to hold on to what he had been given. But he didn't know what to do with himself, either.

As a new generation of extreme athletes dreamt up new ways to use skis to carve their names into *The Guinness Book of World Records*, Dag's place in the sport's lore began to fade. By the 1980s Dag was hardly even skiing anymore. He was living with his family in a two-storey home with a carport next to the Squamish River. He had replaced the Firebird with a Vandura, which he used to ferry his family around. And when he wasn't with his family he was usually logging. Whatever time he did have for sports he generally spent running.

Though he had grown up running long distances on the trails that cut through the forests of Hovlandsmoen, he didn't compete in any organized races until his early 30s, when he finished his first marathon in a pair of jeans. That's when he also started keeping a daily journal. Originally it was a means of keeping track of his training times. But soon it became a record of every day of his life.

"When I started running, people looked at me like I was crazy," Dag said. "People didn't just go out for a run back then. It wasn't really a thing. Most people didn't even own running shoes. It wasn't at all like it is today." Just as skiing had experienced a boom during the 1960s, running experienced its own boom in the late 1970s. Until then, many people in North America didn't understand the health benefits of jogging. In the years that followed, an estimated 30 million Americans suddenly began running for health and recreation. Soon towns across America were

Dag ran his first marathon in a pair of jeans. He got more serious about running as he aged and began to focus more on his finishing times, which helped him track his own aging. By the early 1980s he was competing in multiple endurance tests, including some that mixed skiing and running together.
(Whistler Question Collection, courtesy of the Whistler Museum)

hosting marathons and races of varying lengths. Running shoe companies like Reebok, Nike and New Balance (which in 1972 had just six employees making 30 pairs of shoes a day) exploded with the demand, becoming multinational corporations.

By 1980, running had become as much a part of Dag's life as skiing ever was. He was a running zealot, compulsively logging distances and times onto charts that he kept in binders that began to stack on top of one another as the years wore on. His shirtless presence became a fixture on the streets of Squamish, but also on the rugged mountain terrain that encircled the city. Golden-haired and sporting a handlebar moustache, he looked like he had transplanted Hulk Hogan's face onto Patrick Swayze's frame. Most people didn't pay any attention as they passed him by, but those who did often stopped to ask him if he needed a ride somewhere. Over time Dag's presence on the streets began to inspire a conversion among locals who, after watching him run day after day eventually started to join him, if only for a kilometre or two. Among his earliest converts was a South African émigré named Mabel "Mae" Palm, who was 37 when she first left her house and fell into step behind him. Palm's mother had put her on a plane at age 16 and gotten her out of the apartheid state with enough money to survive a week in London. After joining Dag, she became a running fixture in her own right, completing over 100 marathons, a number of triathlons, 13 Iron Man competitions and several ultras over the next 30 years. She always credited Dag with inspiring her to start running.

As the 1980s wore on, Dag began cutting his own trails through the backwoods that surrounded the city. And though he was happiest when he was alone in nature and without a single other human in sight, he was still a young father who cherished the moments when he could take his children into the forest and run together as a family.

Reflecting on his childhood years later, Dag's son, Hans, remarked that if they could have frozen themselves in place in Squamish, they could have preserved what kept them together as a family. "My father always said, 'Happiness is just a moment in time.' There's something to that."

IT WAS NEVER quite clear to his family whether Dag quit or got fired from his logging job after 18 years. The family generally agreed that he was already drinking heavily by that point, but he hadn't yet inherited the money that would send him into a downward spiral. He was newly unemployed in the summer of 1989, when he and Tony began talking about moving out of Squamish. They no longer needed to be near the logging camps that lined the BC coast and they were spending less and less time up at Whistler. The resort was growing fast and locked in a competition for ticket sales against Blackcomb, which had opened as a rival ski slope in 1980 with the financial backing of the Aspen Skiing Company. The more people flocked to the ski resort, the less Dag cared to be there.

Together, he and Tony spent the early 1980s

paying off the mortgage on their house, and by 1985 they owned their home outright. Then Dag's time as a logger came to an abrupt end. He had little in the way of retirement savings and still needed to work to bring in money for the family. So he went into business as a self-employed tree topper, though he never put much effort into acquiring clients. Then the couple decided to uproot the family and relocate inland to the Okanagan Valley. They sold their home in Squamish and purchased a hillside bungalow in Oyama overlooking a majestic lake surrounded by peach groves and cherry orchards. "I never quite understood the move," Hans recalled. "It seemed impulsive. Squamish was a great place to grow up. I wasn't happy moving, but we had no choice. In Oyama, there was nothing there. I went from being in a class of 30 in Squamish to a class of 10 in Oyama. I was in sixth grade. That was hard."

COUNTLESS TIMES OVER the past 20 years Hans Aabye has tried to make sense of the factors that led to his parents' breakup, the steady unravelling of their family and the destitution of his father. Hans is cautious when speaking with strangers about the full effect his father's life has had on his own. He himself is a competitive marathoner who has many of the same physical attributes as his father. He is tall and slim and he possesses the preternatural ability to run extreme long distances. For years after his parents' divorce, he was the closest thing his father had to a running partner. He speaks of his father affectionately to others, but struggles now to communicate with the man himself. He reveals the pain of being Dag's son, not in the words he speaks, but in his intonation. His voice cracks as he tries to explain why it's okay if he never sees or hears from his father for the rest of his life.

"He is still my father, but circumstances forced me to leave him," Hans told me. "I haven't seen him in 10 years."

It took a while for Hans to understand that the money his father inherited caused more harm to the family than good. But by the time he figured that out, his parents were already living in separate homes and barely communicating.

Shortly after Dag returned to Canada as the unexpected heir to Helga's vast fortune, he and Tony drove north from their new home to Silver Star Mountain, the site of an Okanagan ski resort with rustic charm. They had made frequent trips to the mountain in previous years, rekindling their shared bond over skiing in a place that had significantly smaller crowds than Whistler. On this particular trip they saw a cabin for sale at the base of the resort and decided to use a portion of Dag's inheritance to buy it. The wooden A-frame wasn't big or luxurious, but it was the perfect family getaway, conveniently located so close to the base of the mountain that Dag, Tony and their three teenaged children could ski or walk from their front door to the resort's main ski lift.

The mountain didn't offer anywhere near the same vertical drop as Whistler, but what it lacked in elevation it made up for in snowfall, averaging seven metres a year. Though people had been skiing on Silver Star since the 1930s, the amenities remained rudimentary into the early 1980s, when a business cohort headed by Judd Buchanan, a former minister in Pierre Trudeau's cabinet, set out to convert the mountain into a tourist attraction that would appeal to a different clientele than Whistler. If Whistler and Aspen were the Paris of ski hills, then Silver-Star Resort was more like Dawson City. As the *New York Times* described it in one write-up, the "one-street village includes board sidewalks and Victorian storefronts that have a storybook feel to them" and was "trimmed to look like a turn-of-the-20th-century mining town."

For a brief time the cabin was a home away from home for the entire Aabye family, the gateway to a winter wonderland barely an hour's drive from the orchards that surrounded their home in Oyama. At some point, however, Dag stopped heading back to Oyama altogether. The rest of his family would return home at the end of a weekend to attend school and work, but Dag would stay behind at the mountain. The cabin became a shrine to the man he used to be. The walls were decorated with memorabilia from his ski career. Black-and-white photos from his time at Geilo, La Parva and Whistler hung next to cut-out ads from his modelling days for cigarettes in South America, Fujifilm in the US and ski clothing for Eaton's in Canada. Ski posters for *Ski West*, *Four Faces of Garibaldi* and other films in which he starred also decorated the walls. Race bibs were tacked on the walls next to magazine and newspaper articles about the "Father of Freeride" and the "world's first extreme skier."

At first Tony thought Dag just wanted to hang back and ski. She didn't realize how many days he spent alone at the bars that were all walking distance from the cabin. Those who lived and worked at the base of the mountain remember Dag as a man who would drink heavily, then pull out a wad of money and pay his tab. If there was anyone else still in the bar, he would pay theirs too. According to those who saw him in the bars regularly, he was a generous, if self-destructive, man who seemed to have an endless supply of money and a drinking problem. It took a while for Tony to notice the money disappearing from their account. But it didn't take long for more than $100,000 to disappear. "He just dwindled it away," she said. After that he managed to cover a few of his bar tabs with oil paintings and other keepsakes, and when he could no longer pawn those off as currency he started dipping into the money Tony was bringing in as a care aide. She could see it disappearing from the bank account. "I would work and he would just spend the money," she said. "He would spend $250 a night at the bar. There was nothing I could do."

After more than a year largely living a separate life from Dag and watching her own income disappear, she went to see a lawyer. "It got so bad that I didn't know how much money I had," she said, "because I would be making money and he would spend it. I just thought, we can't do this anymore. I went to legal aid and started the process for the divorce. All I wanted was to divide it. We had a house and a cabin—they were worth the same value. I thought it would be simple. We could just split it in half."

The divorce left the family deeply divided. Dag and Tony's eldest daughter stayed with Tony in Oyama, finished her schooling and has hardly spoken with her father since. The twins were more forgiving. Hans tried for a while to remain close to both his mother and his father. Though he, too, stayed at the house in Oyama, he would head to the cabin to visit his father on weekends. The two stayed tight for more than a decade after the divorce. Dag's youngest daughter was the only one who lived with him after the divorce. She moved into the cabin and watched her father descend into economic despair before her eyes. With no job, and apparently in the midst of some sort of personal crisis, he was soon unable to afford heat or electricity. Dag told her not to worry, that he could still keep them warm and fed. All they needed was the wood stove. For days he tried to keep them both fed on an ever-shrinking diet of flour flapjacks. She didn't want to leave him. She was still young, but she was old enough to know that she needed more support than he was able to provide.

She stayed with him as long as she could. But she was gone by the time he lost the cabin.

NINETEEN

THE PSYCHOLOGY OF REINVENTION

*When we believe something is
beautiful, then it is.*
—DAG'S JOURNALS

The more I got to know of Dag's family life, the more I began to understand that his entire bushman existence had come at the expense of his family and as a result of his own self-destructive tendencies. His wife had left him, two of his children weren't speaking to him, and it wasn't clear whether his eldest child, the one born out of a short-lived romance in Chile, even knew he existed. He had never met any of his grandchildren, and I suspected that he probably never would. He possessed very little in life other than the sentimental keepsakes that he managed to stuff into his bus. It was hard, sometimes, to view his situation as anything other than tragic. And yet Dag insisted that he was the wealthiest, most fortunate man on the planet. He had no interest in anyone's pity. No interest in their charity either.

"I don't waste my time feeling sorry for myself," he told me. "People look at me and say, 'Poor you, you have nothing.' But the most important things in life aren't things at all. Everything I want is right here in front of me. I have wind, I have rain, I have snow, I have sun. So what if I don't have a big home and a big car? I know many people with those things and they still aren't happy.

"If people concentrated more on who they actually are and why they are as they are, they wouldn't need to feel sorry for themselves or for anyone else. The most important person that you need to understand in this life is yourself. You can't begin to understand others if you don't yet understand yourself."

No matter how much Dag talked about his own contentment living alone in a bus in the forest, his words never made it any easier to reconcile what others had told me: that his penurious solitude was the result of unchecked alcohol use and a festering trauma that traced back to his childhood. The more time I spent with him, the more I began to see how and why the members of his family had chosen to walk away from him. And yet I remained drawn to him. Or, more specifically, to the perpetually positive way he viewed the world.

His family said his drinking had become increasingly problematic after Helga died. But Dag never accepted that. He said he liked to drink beer, but he didn't believe he had a drinking problem or that his alcohol use may have damaged his relationship with his wife or with any of his children. Nor did he believe he had wasted his inheritance. He said he had given large sums of money away because he didn't really want it. He didn't understand why anyone would fault him for that. In Dag's version of events, alcohol and in-laws had played a role in the divorce, but it wasn't his drinking and it wasn't his parents that caused the rifts within the family. He didn't blame Tony for leaving him. He understood that she had to do what she thought was best for her. But he didn't really acknowledge that his children had drifted away from him after the divorce. He often repeated how important it was that he never become an embarrassment to his children. It was never quite clear to me whether he understood that his eldest daughter wanted nothing to do with him or that his son hadn't spoken to him in more than a decade. Whenever he spoke of either of them, he made it sound as if he had just talked to them. For the first few years I knew him I actually believed that he kept in touch with both of them. But then I realized that the stories he told about them were all 10 to 20 years old. He refused to acknowledge that neither of them had been in touch in years, and he was either unable or unwilling to acknowledge the circumstances that led to their falling out. Over our many interviews, I pressed him on this, but he preferred not to talk about it or simply ignored the question. He spoke of his children's accomplishments with pride and never let on that anything had ever been broken between them. He was unfailingly optimistic about everything. Even when discussing his own pain or misfortune.

One time, as we sat by a fire in the bush, he told me how, shortly after Tony left him, someone had broken into and stolen the Vandura. He took the theft as a blessing. After all, he didn't have any money to insure the van, service it or keep it fuelled. By the time he noticed it was missing, he couldn't even remember the last time he had seen it, let alone driven it. He didn't care enough to report the theft to police.

When he told me this story, it came out sounding like a parable. There was a moral at its end, a lesson to be learned. He said: "After the van was stolen, I stood in the parking lot and said, 'Thank you, thief!'"

"Why would you thank the thief?" I asked.

He replied: "Because whoever stole the van liberated me of one more thing I did not want or need."

A lot of Dag's stories were like that. He would recount something bad that had happened to him without expressing any sadness or anger. I found myself wishing I could see the world the way Dag saw it because he found beauty in everything. As one of his friends, Sarah, a bus driver who had come to know him as the quiet old passenger who often climbed aboard the bus on the edge of one forest and rode it to the edge of another, explained: "Dag is a master of neuroplasticity. His mind has this incredible ability to rewire things that you and I see as negative and view them instead as some sort of positive."

Sarah had met Dag about a year after I did. She struck up a conversation with him one day after giving him a ride on her bus. "I was curious about him from the very first time I picked him up," she said. "He was unique and mysterious. I always wondered where he was coming from and where he was going." She could see everything that happened on the bus through the rear-view mirror. She watched over and over as her other passengers got on the bus, took one look at Dag, gave him a wide berth and sat at the opposite end of the bus. She could see that people tended to avoid him because of his appearance. It bothered her, even though it clearly didn't bother him. One day, when he was the only passenger, she walked to the back, sat down beside him and asked him his name. Soon they were hiking partners, and for a time she was his closest friend. She would accompany him on long treks to the top of cliffs and together they would pitch a tent and stay there overnight, watching the sun rise over the valley below. He was 77 and she was several years his junior. She would leave him messages along his trails and they would meet by one of his firepits and talk the night away. Then one day she stopped leaving him messages and stopped coming by altogether. He missed her, but he understood she didn't really want to be with him anymore. So he carried on running and hiking and camping in the forest by himself.

I visited him shortly after Sarah had left him. He was unfazed by the loss, and when I asked him how he was doing emotionally, he said that all things in life can be a blessing if you look at them the right way. Then he jumped into another parable about the time he had fallen so far behind on his hydro bills at the cabin after Tony left him that the electric company cut off the power. "I learned something about myself when the power went out," he said. "I learned that I really prefer to cook over an open fire."

He could see by the confusion on my face that I was struggling to find the moral of that story, so he tried to spell it out more clearly. "Whenever you lose something, you gain something at the same time," he said. "Maybe it's freedom. Maybe it's knowledge. But if all you ever do is focus on what's been lost, then you'll never appreciate what you actually have."

He paused while I completed the mental gymnastics required to follow his train of thought. Then he started into another story, this one about how, after the hydro was shut off and the cold set in and he had been surviving on nothing but flapjacks, he fell so far behind on the property taxes and alimony payments to Tony that she went to court and sold the cabin that he had been living in. It was the first time I had heard him recount, in any honesty, how his own actions had led to his own impoverishment, and the closest he ever came in my presence to criticizing his ex-wife.

"Do you regret what happened to you?" I asked.

"How could I?" he replied. "Look at the life I live. There is beauty in everything. You just have to find it."

The story of how Dag wound up living in a bus—the real story, devoid of any recasting of negatives into positives—is a thoughtful story of love and charity, forgiveness and chance. It's the story of how several key figures in the SilverStar community rallied together to drag a 30-year-old yellow Bluebird International school bus into the forest so that Dag could live out his days in relative peace away from the scrutiny of those who viewed him as a vagrant.

His friends at SilverStar had watched in bewilderment as Dag drank for hours in the village's bars at night only to see him again at dawn, seemingly sober and first in line at the chairlift. Dag attracted attention to himself every time he went down the hill. Sometimes it was because he had on only one ski. Other times it was because he was downhill skiing on cross-country skis with no edges. He set a record for the most double black diamonds skied in a day (31), and continued to ski over cliffs and under chairlifts where no one else would even think to ski. Eventually the people running the resort decided to name one of their most difficult trails Aabye Road. In the early days at SilverStar, he dabbled in speed skiing, rocketing down the hill at over 140 kilometres an hour while wearing an airtight rubber jumpsuit, trying to see if he could make it in a sport that was considered too dangerous for the Olympics.

When the snow melted away Dag took up mountain biking, completing three 24-hour relays as a solo contestant, one year with his arm in a cast. The speed skiing and mountain biking put him back on the radar of the extreme sporting community. Soon newspapers and ski magazines near and far were writing stories about the return of the "Father of Freeride." But the stories, even those written by reporters who actually travelled to SilverStar to see him in the flesh, missed the fact that Dag's life was crumbling around him.

By the mid-1990s, Dag could no longer afford a lift pass or his own equipment. He became less of a presence on the slopes and at the bars, and by the winter of 1996 he was surviving on a diet of flour and water, which he moulded together and fried on an open fire inside his cabin.

Among the first people to express concern for his wellbeing was Brian James, a former ski instructor who met Dag at Banff's Sunshine Village in 1969. In the mid-1990s, Brian was running a ski shop at the base of Silver Star. He watched as an increasingly emaciated Dag trained endlessly for cross-country ski races, only to show up at the start line with gear that was either antiquated or damaged beyond repair. Brian felt for Dag every time and sensed that his old friend's training was integral to keeping him alive. "I think some of the training may have been a means of escape," he said. Brian found it sad, though, to see Dag train so hard for competition and then struggle in the actual race because he couldn't afford half-decent gear. "Dag was a really proud guy," recalled Brian, "so I couldn't just give him gear. He didn't want that. I used to get him to 'test' stuff for me, as a way to get him on better gear so that he could really compete and do his best."

With Brian supplying the gear, Dag managed to reinvent himself into a Canadian champion cross-country skier. He was still thin and malnourished when, at the age of 61, he qualified for the world championships in Quebec City. In February 2002, with the support of his friends at SilverStar, he flew across the country with his skis, boots, poles and a bag of clothes. When he got to Quebec City, he checked himself into a youth hostel, where he waxed his gear before making his way to the race to compete against skiers from around the world. He finished fourth in his age group, then flew home.

When he arrived back at SilverStar, he focused his energy on using his fitness levels to assert his independence. He would routinely run 25 kilometres from Silver Star village down into Vernon, only to turn around and run back. "He would never stick his thumb out," recalled Brian. "He was always totally mobile.

"I think he became the runner we later came to know partly out of necessity, partly out of an urge to remain as independent as he could be under the circumstances, and partly out of an urge not to grow old. When you've been in a business like skiing, there's two ways of growing old. You either keep fit, and that keeps you mobile, or you slowly lose the agility and lose the flexibility and strength to keep it going. Somewhere in there, when he was 55 or 60, I don't know if he hit rock bottom, but he developed this philosophy that it was a gift and a privilege to be able to do what he does. To be able to ski and to run and to enjoy nature, versus someone who hops in a car and has to drive to work for 90 minutes to sit at a desk. He really made a point of appreciating the natural things in life that he did have.

"Some people see him as an innocent. I see him as having made a decision at some point, maybe when he lost what possessions he had, maybe he hit that point where he said, 'I don't need all these trappings in life, I'm just going to look after me and run where I want to run and spend time with those who want to spend time with me. And if nobody wants to spend time with me, then I'll spend time by myself.'"

While Brian outfitted Dag with the gear required to continue skiing competitively, the husband-and-wife owners of a deli at the base of the mountain worked together to orchestrate Dag's salvation. In 1997, Denys Lawrence and his wife, Monika, hired Dag to work as a dishwasher. It was a gateway job for Dag, who would later work at a local food bank, earning enough to eat until he reached 65 and began collecting old age security.

Dag was an idiosyncratic dishwasher, prone to long conversations with those who came into the deli or the food bank looking for a sandwich. Despite working an honest job, he did not adhere to the usual social contract. He didn't pay his property taxes (this was one of the reasons he lost the cabin), didn't file any child support (Tony had managed to garnishee his wages for a brief time when he worked as a tree planter before taking the job at the deli), let his driver's licence, health card and all other government-issued ID lapse, and showed up to only one court hearing during the seven years that it took for the courts to process his divorce.

"There was something within Dag that seemed to be missing," Denys remarked. "He didn't seem to feel that he owed anything to anyone."

When Dag lost his cabin it looked as though

he was destined to live on the street. For a time, he slept in the laundry room of the hotel that also housed the deli. Denys knew that Dag was either unable or unwilling to plot a path toward financial salvation, and as another winter began to set in at Silver Star, he began to worry.

One day Denys learned that an itinerant tree planter down in the valley was selling a school bus that had been converted into something of an RV. The bus that would become Dag's home had arrived in BC by way of Quebec, where it had served out its initial purpose through the 1970s before being sold to a young nomad named Scotty, who ripped out the bench seats and installed a bed and kitchenette before driving it across the country. When Scotty arrived in the Okanagan, he parked the bus in the valley and went into the hills to plant trees. When the kid decided he wanted to continue onward to Asia, he began looking for someone to buy the bus. As a vehicle, the bus was nearing the end of its life. The frame and body were rusting out and the engine was in need of a rebuild. But as a shelter, it had potential. Denys offered Scotty $3,000 and drove the bus back to SilverStar, where he handed Dag the keys.

Dag kept the bus parked in a lot at the base of the ski hill. For a few weeks, he drove it in and out of town. Then the motor seized and he couldn't afford to fix it. What money he had from washing dishes he spent on plywood and lumber and transformed its inside into what would become his forever home. The bus already contained a wood stove, but it had no insulation and needed a new chimney. Dag cut a hole through the roof, installed a chimney, built a bedroom in the back and lined the bus's steel walls and flooring with wood for added insulation. Then he installed another wall behind the driver's seat and a kitchenette. Though he had lost all his furniture along with the cabin, he had managed to save his old journals, as well as the portraits of his children and framed photos from his days at Whistler, La Parva and elsewhere. He hung them on the walls of the bus.

For two years the bus sat in one of the resort's main lots. Skiers would pull into the lot and park next to the rusted-out yellow bus, smoke often rising out of its chimney. Sometimes Dag would be inside reading or sleeping or chronicling the day's events in his journals. Most days he preferred to be away in the forest when the crowds arrived. But the constant presence of a decrepit old smoking school bus in the parking lot, and Dag wandering in and out of the bush to relieve himself, were enough to wear out his welcome. By the spring of 2001, the resort had been sold, and the new owners were eager to get rid of both Dag and his yellow eyesore.

The new owners didn't care that there were ski runs named after Dag on the mountainside. Or that he had spent two years hand-cutting a 12-kilometre trail system through the forest, connecting pedestrians from the village to the peak via a majestic winding path that blended routes used by animals and routes used by miners of old and would eventually be signposted and added to the resort's trail map.

For a while, the new owners threatened to tow the bus away with or without Dag inside. He didn't protest the eviction, but he didn't know where to go, either. Then one of the groomer operators, who owned 30 acres of wild bush halfway down the mountainside, told Dag that if he could find a way to drag the bus onto his property, he could carry on living out of sight, out of mind in part of the forest where nobody would ever bother him.

Dag battened down whatever he could inside the bus. Then he watched as a big-rig tow truck lifted his home off the ground and transported it down the mountain, turned onto a gravel road and carried the old bus as deep into the forest as it could go. And just when he thought the tow truck couldn't get it any farther, he watched as the driver hooked a winch to the back of the bus, looped it around a distant trunk and dragged it to its final resting space next to a brush of wild cedars.

It was early spring and he was now all alone in the bus halfway between the city of Vernon and the village at the base of Silver Star. Outside the snow was melting. The forest animals were rustling. Dag stepped out of the bus with a chainsaw over his shoulder and set out to cut a path to nothing and nowhere in particular.

TWENTY

NEVER DIE EASY

How many things there are that I do not want.
—SOCRATES, QUOTED IN DAG'S JOURNALS

To make sense of the person Dag came to represent online and in people's minds, you have to decide for yourself who he was to begin with. And to do that you have to reconcile for yourself whether to give more credence to the narrative of his life as Dag preferred to tell it, as the media chose to portray it or as those closest to him understood it. Regardless, you are left with some contradictory mélange of archetypes all rolled into one human being. Outlaw. Sage. Explorer. Innocent. You get Dag the mythological hermit—a wise old man, living in a veritable mountain cave tucked in the forest. But you are also left with Dag the innocent fool, less in the Shakespearean style and more like the fool from a deck of tarot cards—unconventional and unorthodox, devoid of restraints or commitments.

And then you get Dag the tortured tragic hero of Grecian tradition, a flawed soul beset by grave misfortune as a result of his own actions. He is Brontë's Heathcliff. He is Marvel's Wolverine. He is Spielberg's stranded alien. He is Dag from the forest. Son of mystery. Father of freeride. All the archetypes are there—but the whole will always end up as less than the sum of its parts. Because mixed in among those parts are realities that are impossible to ignore. The more time I spent with Dag, the more I noticed the myriad differences between his view of who he was and what he was doing on this earth and the views of everyone else around him.

I wondered if perhaps what his friend Sarah had labelled his "neuroplasticity" was actually more in line with what Marlene Steinberg, a psychiatrist and researcher at Yale University, describes as dissociation—"an adaptive defence in response to high-stress trauma characterized by memory loss and a sense of disconnection from oneself or one's surroundings." And I wondered if perhaps his unwillingness to let anything break his spirit was ultimately a greater attribute than his physicality.

Most days, however, I simply wished I could see the world as Dag saw it. There was no room for pity, remorse or pain in Dag's mind. No time for anger or resentment, either. It was as if he had found some way to clear those emotions from his limbic system. But there were other times when Dag's view of his world conflicted so greatly with everyone else's that it wasn't clear if he was even experiencing life in the same way as the rest of us. Rarely did he seem more disconnected from his reality than when he spoke of his children as if he had just seen them, even though years had passed since their last encounter.

"The most important thing for any parent is that you never be a burden to your children." It was a line he repeated to me time and again over the course of our friendship. It always reminded me of something Hans had told me the one time I met him.

"My father's independence is his greatest strength," Hans had said. "But it's also his greatest weakness. When the time comes, I don't believe he will call on any of us for help. I think he'll go somewhere alone to not be found. And then he will die."

Despite all the focus Dag put on living as independently as possible, exercising religiously, climbing up unnamed mountains to sit alone on the edge of society, refusing rides to and from town, and dissociating himself from all but the most basic commitments to humanity, not to mention to his family (both his adoptive one in Norway and the one he had created in Canada), he was never really fully independent.

For 20 years he lived in the bus, rent-free, on another man's land. Dag was 75 years old when that man finally grew tired of having him and his bus parked on his land and told him that it was time to move along. Their relationship soured over the next five years as it became clear that Dag wasn't leaving, not just because the bus could no longer move, but because he didn't really have anywhere else to go. He forestalled his own eviction by refusing to acknowledge that he and his bus technically existed on private property where he was no longer welcome. The bus could not easily be moved and therefore neither could he. Those were the facts of Dag's situation, but Dag insisted the truth was that he was free. In his mind, his lack of material possessions granted him more freedom than most people enjoyed. He didn't refer to his bus as his home. He said the forest was his home, and the bus was just his preferred shelter. He literally viewed it as a lair or a cave. Doing so allowed him to see himself as more nomadic than homeless. Over time I came to understand that even though others may have viewed him as a prisoner of circumstance trapped by his economic misfortune, the view he had of himself was really all that mattered.

He refused to feel sorry for himself and held no ill will toward anyone for anything that had happened to him. When I asked him if he resented having been pushed into the forest by those who didn't want to see him in their parking lot, Dag turned the question around, making his response less about the people who shooed him away and more of a parable about forgiveness and nature. "People say nature is unforgiving," he said. "But it is the most forgiving home I have ever known."

Dag's naivety, wilful or not, made him one of the most difficult subjects I had ever tried to write about. He always struck me as intensely honest, even when he was telling stories that didn't seem plausible. Tony articulated this simply and concisely when she said to me: "Dag has the most innocent mind I've ever known." But there was so much more to him than just innocence. It was never lost on me that a lesser man would have been broken by the circumstances of Dag's life, and yet Dag could not even bring himself to say anything bad about anyone or anything. Not about the family members who had disowned him as an adult, nor the ones who had abused and abandoned him as a child, nor the countless members of society who looked at him as nothing more than a wanderer. From an early age, Dag had this remarkable inability to express anger, jealousy, pettiness or any of the usual negative traits that overcome a human during times of intense struggle.

As COMPLEX AS the man was, it was the oversimplified legend of Dag the mysterious old trail runner and mountain man that led filmmakers and journalists like me to fly to the Okanagan and head into the forest to seek him out. It appeared to all of us that Dag had become this legendary figure unconsciously. He had transformed himself from aging ski bum into ageless ultramarathon runner because he needed to remain active simply to survive in the space he inhabited. He hadn't set out to accomplish anything that might attract anyone's attention when he began training for his first Death Race.

He remembered very well the day that transformation began. It was in 2003, and Dag was just beginning his 20-year hermitage. It was not quite spring and snow could still be found in the shade of the spruce and the cedar and the tall white pine when his son, Hans, came to visit with a flyer in his hand. Hans had heard of a 125-kilometre ultramarathon in northern Alberta that he thought he himself might try to run and which he believed his father might find challenging. "Here's something you're probably too old to do," Hans said. He gave Dag the flyer. "They call it the Death Race," Hans said. "It's pretty much the most extreme endurance race in Canada." Dag looked over the flyer and tucked the details into his mind. He never spoke to his son about how challenging the previous few years had been. He didn't think Hans needed to know all the boring aspects of his day-to-day existence.

When Hans left, Dag began his first day of training for an event that would come to define the next two decades of his life. Over the years that followed, he remained largely oblivious that his annual appearance at the Death Race had created a legend that grew online through posts and photos of this mysterious old man who lived to run and ran to live. In the eyes of those who did not know him, he was a superathlete who lived off the grid and refused to grow old.

As the years passed, the least interesting thing about Dag was that he had once been in a James Bond movie. When journalists came looking for him, they came in search of a man they would later portray as the oldest extreme athlete on the planet. The narratives all told the story of a Norwegian ski star turned Hollywood stuntman who became a vagabond trail runner. Sometimes the journalists treated Dag like some kind of wild animal, best to be admired in his natural habitat. Other times they treated him like an enlightened old mystic. Dag didn't pay much attention to the coverage until the stories became inescapable.

IN THE MORE than 20 years that Dag spent living in his old bus on the side of a mountain, he came to represent a great many things to a great many people, especially after an online video of him went viral in the spring of 2018. The film had been recorded the previous summer. Dag, 76 years old at the time, was followed by two filmmakers from Vancouver who launched a drone over his trails and caught up with him at the bus. Then they left, and he carried on training for that year's Death Race. What more than 1.7 million people knew of him was filtered through the lens of that 14-minute video, which labelled him "the most elusive man in North America." The film captured only a fraction of who he was and projected an image of Dag to the world that few people who knew him recognized as being true. What the film did capture, though, was that Dag was a human enigma whose legend grew the longer he spent living, and running, in the relative solitude of the backcountry of British Columbia.

As the summer of 2017 wore on, forest fires

set in all over the province, impeding his journey to Grand Cache. For the first time in 15 years, he didn't make it to the race. Then came the autumn and the grouse that startled him on the trail and the fall that wrecked his shoulder, followed by the blood poisoning over Christmas while he was convalescing. By February 2018 he was back at the bus, trying to regain what he had lost. He wasn't entirely sure what his body was capable of anymore. He could take to the trails and run for hours without rest, but he was moving slower than before and covering significantly less ground.

He was struggling to get back up to speed when those same filmmakers who had followed him with a drone months earlier uploaded their short film onto the internet. Soon images of Dag sitting outside his bus and running on his trails were being shared around the world. He had no idea this was going on until he noticed strangers had begun to point at him when he ran down into town. He knew about the internet, but he had never gone online and had no idea what it meant to "go viral." He knew what social media was because he had read about it over the years, but he didn't fully understand or appreciate that while he had been leading an increasingly disconnected life, the rest of the world was becoming increasingly connected. It was all very abstract.

He had just run into town and was waiting for

a bus that would take him toward another training ground when a man and a woman walking by shouted out his name. Dag looked absently at the two strangers staring at him.

"You're the guy from the video," the woman said. Then she pulled out her phone and snapped a photo of him as he stood confused on the side of the road.

The filmmakers had titled their short *Never Die Easy*, after the words on a coffee mug that Dag kept at the bus. The first eight minutes chronicled the journey of two young men as they set out to find Dag in the middle of the BC backcountry. They described him as a complete solitarian, like an uncontacted Amazonian tribesman. More than a million people had already watched the film within days of its posting. By the time Dag became aware of its existence, it was being shared all over Facebook and Twitter and other social media sites. *The Atlantic*, *Men's Journal* and *Outside* magazine had all linked to the film, sharing it on their own websites and perpetuating the image of Dag as an elusive hermit. "Aabye is a rare breed of human that has lived his own path and blown the doors off the perception of what life has to be," *Men's Journal* declared.

In the film, a feral-looking Dag summarizes what nearly two decades living in a bus has done to his mindset. "Life is a gift," he says to the camera. "To me there is no age, it's just life. You know, age is something other people will put on you . . . To me, I don't have an age.

"I'm perfectly imperfect," he concludes. "Tomorrow, I want to be a better person than today. You can always work on yourself. And if you work on yourself you don't have time to talk about other people or worry about other people . . . I don't try to understand people . . . The only person you want to understand, really, is yourself."

The film simultaneously polarized and captivated those who watched it. Soon, people from all over the world were commenting on Dag's life. Some thought the film was cheesy. Others thought Dag was idiotic. Most, however, found his way of life inspiring. Locals he had never met were now trying to locate the bus. A brewery in the Okanagan latched on to the story and named a beer after Dag, while the organizers of multiple ultramarathons in the United States began sending him invitations to compete at their races as an honoured guest.

The video had been circulating for about a month when someone forwarded it to my mother. She had just finished her first round of chemotherapy. She called me immediately and asked if this was the same guy who had called me from a payphone in a Walmart parking lot when I was visiting her once.

"Same guy," I told her.

"Did you ever find his mother?" she asked.

"Not yet," I said.

"You better hurry up," she said. "Time catches up with everyone. He can't possibly live like that much longer."

My mother was 72 years old at the time and had just gone through a lumpectomy for an aggressive cancer that, unbeknownst to her, had already spread to her brain. Despite the cancer, she was actually in good shape for her age and remained physically active, though she suffered from degenerative disc disease in her lower back, carpal tunnel syndrome in her wrists and osteoarthritis in one knee. She had undergone knee surgery at the age of 70 so that she could get back to her routine of long walks without pain and had no sooner recovered when she found a lump on her breast. We had spoken almost every day since her cancer diagnosis. We talked about life, about family and about whatever story I was working on. She was always fascinated about the people I wrote about. She would pepper me with questions about their motivations and mine. What attracted me to them? What made them open up their lives to a journalist like me? Most times she was satisfied just to hear me try to explain to her why they did what they did, lived where they lived and loved what they loved. But there was one thing about Dag that had stuck with her when I shared his story. It was the way he managed to recast everything in his life as a positive. He had once told me that the secret to surviving even the harshest ordeal was to live by the motto of "No bad days." I shared that with my mother early on during her chemotherapy. She repeated it back to me weeks later, when she was too ill to even get out of bed. "No bad days," she said. Then she asked after my "ageless friend who lives in a bus."

"I hope you can help him find what he's looking for," she said.

"So do I," I replied.

I had no idea then that I would spend large parts of the next year trying to help him find his mother. Or that while doing so, I would lose mine.

TWENTY-ONE

HIDDEN IN THE PAST

*It's the black spots on your life
that haunt you in the dark.*

—ANONYMOUS QUOTE IN DAG'S JOURNALS

Leafing through decades of Dag's journals, I began to understand what it meant to see his life the way he saw it. His journals were meticulous in their recording of the moments that make up both a day and a life. He took the time, every day, to reflect on the beauty behind the most mundane things imaginable. Every cup of coffee, every sunrise, every sunset. Every rainy morning, every snowy night. Every lonely, meditative run. Every sweet hello, every long goodbye, every kind stranger's deliberate gesture. He used his journal to reflect on all of it. If someone gifted him a sandwich on the road, he wrote it down, describing everything from the taste to the sentiments that emerged from that simple action. The more I read, the more I realized how easy it was to lose sight of the moments that make up a day, let alone the days that make up a year or the years that make up a life.

"My wealth is not in what I have but how I feel." He had written that line on a cold and quiet morning in March 2018, amid details of the starry sky he had seen at 4:30 while fetching wood to feed the fire that would keep him from freezing before the dawn. He had followed that line with another: *"The first day of the rest of my life,"* he wrote. *"Another beautiful day coming on . . . I'm pretty lucky living here."* Day after day, the journals were filled with the same positivity that he always expressed in conversation.

When I first met Dag, I hoped to eventually tell his story by tracking the rise and fall of a life riddled with tragic complexity, and to understand how it all fit together from the start. I thought I could draw it out from birth to present, uncover a narrative line, isolating the real from the imaginary, without disrupting the natural fantasy that is memory. But the more I studied his journals and the more I got to know him, the more I realized that Dag never saw his life through such a structured lens. His life, like his journal entries, was punctuated by a mishmash of remembrances with their own tiny morals. He made a habit of trying to record everything that ever happened to him, but he didn't try to draw causal links between one event and another. Another line from another journal: *"Sometimes the most meaningful thing you can do is accept that some things have no meaning."* He didn't pay much attention to consequence, and I wondered where that trait had come from. He was so focused on his own independence that he didn't seem conscious of just how dependent he actually was on other people or how much of an influence (positive or negative) he had on the lives of those who had loved him most throughout his life. He was always adamant that he didn't need anything from anyone, and I wondered how much of that came from his own history of being orphaned as a child.

EVER SINCE OUR first encounter back in late 2015, I had been trying to help Dag solve the mystery at the centre of his existence—the nature of his origin, the identity of his parents. He was intrigued when I told him I thought I could help him. He told me, in one of our earliest conversations, that as far as he knew, his mother had been a young Norwegian living in Oslo when the

Germans invaded. Three months later, she was pregnant. He suspected, though he didn't know for sure, that he had been one of the roughly 8,000 official Lebensborn babies. But he also thought that he could have been one of the estimated 4,000 other undocumented children fathered by German soldiers. He said that there was nothing in life he really wanted except for a photo of his biological mother. Something to hold on to. An image to identify with, a face to study, a reminder that he hadn't just come from somewhere, but from some*one*.

Working from the few details Dag had given me, I began scouring online resources, corresponding with genealogists and archivists in Norway, Sweden and Germany and trying to build profiles of a man and a woman who so far existed in nothing more than a church book. It wasn't much to go on, but I knew that so long as the names were real they should appear in other records—censuses, birth certificates, marriage licences, immigration papers, newspaper clippings and death certificates.

At first, I checked to see if Dag had been an official child of the Lebensborn. Like most Nazi institutions, the Lebensborn kept meticulous records. Children were assigned numbers at birth and a file was opened for each. Inside each file was information about the child's parents, a pseudoscientific registry of Aryan bloodlines. Many of those files survived and were housed at the Norwegian National Archives. Unfortunately, there were no records of Dag Aabye or Erik Hansen in them. The earliest surviving documentation of an official Lebensborn child born in Norway was dated August 24, 1941, three months after Dag was born. It wasn't clear, however, whether that child was the first or just the earliest child with surviving records.

I began searching for more clues, liaising with other Lebensborn children who had gone through the arduous process of discovering their origins. Most had managed to locate their files between the 1990s and mid-2000s. Soon I was engaging with multiple offices of the Norwegian government, but none appeared to have any records of Dag or his birth parents. The more I searched without results, though, the more committed I became to the quest. Dag had been told 27 years earlier, in a letter from the church where he was baptized, that the name listed for his father was believed to be fake, and so he hadn't bothered to remember it. The name that the church had given for his mother, Heda Hansen, proved equally untraceable. There were numerous Heda Hansens living in Norway during the war, but as far as I could tell none had ever registered a son named Erik.

So I doubled back down the same trail Dag had gone down 27 years earlier and I called up the church in Oslo where he was baptized. It took a while for the person there to locate the two-line record of Dag's baptism in a 77-year-old registry book, but when she finally found it she photographed the entry and shared it with me by email. I looked at the handwritten entry and realized immediately why I had been unable to find any trace of Dag's mother. He had been chasing the wrong name. His mother's name, according to the church book, was Hedvig Marie Hansen. It wasn't clear to me whether the church had given Dag the wrong name to begin with or if he had simply misremembered it.

I began placing calls and firing off emails to more contacts in Oslo while combing online databases for any clues as to where Hedvig had come from or where she went after she gave Dag up for adoption. There was little to be found before the German invasion, when, according to Dag's baptismal record, she had lived in a hotel in Oslo. From what I could tell, that hotel had been expropriated by the German military early in the occupation. It wasn't proof that his father was a Nazi soldier, but the evidence seemed to be lining up. I looked again at the records the church in Oslo had sent me. Next to Dag's mother's name was the name that Dag had been told was likely a fake one given to mask the identity of his father. The church book recorded his father's name as Johan Nielsen, born in 1892.

According to the book, Dag's mother was 32 and his father was 49 at the time of his birth. I began searching through historic census data for both Hedvig Marie Hansen and Johan Nielsen. Dag's father didn't show up anywhere. Dag's mother, however, did. She had been born in 1909 in a small village on the southern coast of Norway called Kragerø. Suddenly I knew more about her than Dag ever had.

From the census data I could see that she had grown up in a white clapboard house within sight of the sea. From what I could tell, the house was still there. I also learned that her father was a sailor, and from earlier census data I discovered that her father's father had been a sailor too.

I called up the church in Kragerø where Dag's mother had been baptized 109 years earlier to see if they had any other records and any parish photos from the past. It wasn't clear how old Hedvig had been when she left Kragerø, or whether she had any siblings. The last census data I was able to access said she was an only child living in a modest home that was shared by other families. From what I could piece together, it didn't look like Dag's maternal family had been wealthy. I later learned that Hedvig's childhood had been marked by its own tragedy. She was just seven years old when her father was lost at sea. He was 39 years old and serving as mate on a Norwegian cargo vessel loaded with coal and heading from England to Denmark through hostile waters at the height of the First World War when his ship disappeared. None of the 14 crew members were ever seen again.

It took weeks for me to reconnect with Dag and pass on my findings. He was standing in a Walmart parking lot again, using the payphone, when I told him he had his mother's name wrong and that the woman he had thought was his mother, the one who died in a car accident in Sweden, appeared to have been someone else entirely. He listened quietly as I rewrote the only things he had ever really known about her. I hadn't fathomed that in sharing the truth with him, I would inadvertently be taking away from him what little he believed he knew of his mother. It took a few moments for me to realize what I had just done.

I shared with him everything that I had pieced together of her childhood and of where she had lived at the outbreak of the Second World War. Finally, he asked me a question that was rooted in the first thing he had ever been told about his mother.

"Was she a prostitute?"

"I don't know whether that's true," I said.

"It's okay," Dag said. "And my father?"

"I found a name," I said. "Johan Olav Nielsen. He was born in 1892."

"Johan," Dag said, softly. It seemed to me that he was hearing the name for the first time. It wasn't clear to either of us whether he had been told the name 27 years earlier. "And he died in the war?" Dag asked.

I told him I didn't know but that I was trying to find his military records through the German government. "I'm still trying to figure out what happened to your mother after the war," I said.

There was no record of Hedvig Marie Hansen having been buried in Norway. So I began looking for records outside of Norway, beginning with Sweden. I was at home in Toronto, sitting at my desk surrounded by Dag's journals, when I typed his mother's name into a database called the Swedish Death Book. I got a positive match, and suddenly I was looking at a document that said Dag's mother had died in an apartment in Gothenburg, Sweden, of a peptic ulcer at the age of 62. I began digging deeper.

The death and burial record at the Örgryte parish in Gothenburg offered a little bit more information, though not much. It recorded that Hedvig had been buried 23 days after she died, but it didn't list a gravesite and had no other information on file other than two simple words—"Unmarried woman." At the time of her death, she had lived in an old apartment block in one of Gothenburg's rougher neighbourhoods. It wasn't clear how long she had been there or whether she lived alone. But what was clear is that she had immigrated to Sweden on April 7, 1946—11 months after the German surrender. She arrived alone at the age of 36 and had taken a job as a dishwasher at a historic seaside restaurant that looked out over the Kattegat sea and the Jutland peninsula. She lived for a time in the inn above the restaurant.

So Dag's earlier understanding that his mother had fled the country shortly after the war was true. Though there wasn't documentary evidence that she had been under threat in Oslo after the German surrender, the timing of her arrival in Sweden suggested that she was possibly trying to escape the reprisals that were reserved for women who had either had, or were simply rumoured to have had, relationships with Germans. In Gothenburg, Dag's mother would have been far away from the angry mobs that isolated Norwegian women on the streets of Oslo, where their heads were shaved in public so that they could be easily identified, abused and harassed. If it was true that she had fled to Sweden for this reason, then she got out of Norway just in time. By the end of 1946, many of those who had been accused of sleeping with the enemy were stripped of their citizenship and interned in special camps. Some were ultimately deported to Germany, while others were committed to psychiatric institutions.

It was one week after Dag's 77th birthday, in 2018, when I met him on a gravel road near the bus. I parked my rented Dodge and followed him to a campfire in the forest. There, as we sat and listened to crackling flames, I told him that I had found where his mother was born and where she died.

"I don't know whose family you spoke to on the phone back in 1990," I said, "but I don't believe you found the right one. Your grandfather was a sailor in a seaside village along the coast of Telemark. And your great-grandfather was a sailor too."

"She was born by the sea?"

I nodded.

He looked at me as if his mind was elsewhere. I hadn't learned much about any of them other than their occupations and their dates of birth and death, but to Dag, I had given him a life story for the ones who came before him.

"Did my mother die alone?" he asked.

"I don't know," I said.

I pulled out a copy of the death certificate I had

been sent from an archive in Sweden. He read it over and reflected on the date—October 3, 1971.

I could see him working it through in his mind, trying to figure out where he may have been on that day.

"I had just gotten married," he said. "On the other side of the world."

We both paused and let that realization sink in. Then I broke the silence. "I haven't been able to find a photo of her," I said. "But I have found where she's buried."

"In Norway?" he asked.

"No, Sweden," I said. "Would you like to see it?"

He looked at me, bewildered. "I don't think I can run that far."

TWENTY-TWO

A PRODIGAL SON

Time isn't the main thing. It's the only thing.
—MILES DAVIS, QUOTED IN DAG'S JOURNALS

It took months to get Dag the documentation he required to travel. Getting him an emergency Norwegian passport wasn't so difficult, but getting him documentation to prove that he had been legally in Canada for half a century was significantly more onerous. Without a valid permanent resident card in hand, there was no guarantee that he would be allowed back into Canada if he left the country. I was cautious about creating a scenario that would leave him stranded in some international airport, unable to return to the forest and the mountainside he called home. Dag was 78 years old at the time and, though he was fully capable of making his own decisions, I thought I should first alert at least one of his children to what we were doing. So I called up his youngest daughter. I told her that I had located the site of her grandmother's grave in Sweden and was now trying to locate her grandfather's final resting place too. She was curious about the insights into her family history and listened as I outlined the risks to her father of travelling without proof of his legal residency in Canada. It occurred to me that she might not be keen for me to lead him out of the country. But she said something that stuck with me.

"If you can get him back to Norway it might actually be better for him if he could stay there." It was a sad comment, but it was also incredibly well intentioned and honest, and I understood what she meant by it entirely.

I had been warned by Citizenship and Immigration Canada that because of the complexities of Dag's case, it could take more than a year to process his permanent residency. In the end, it was a 69-year-old ski aficionado and part-time Norwegian honorary consul in Calgary who helped to expedite the process.

Egil Bjørnsen was just a few months away from mandatory retirement when he took my call. He said Dag's consular case was perhaps the most unusual and personal he had worked on during 30 years as an honorary consul. There was something about a man approaching the end of his life without knowing the beginning that really struck Egil. He was determined to help Dag clear up his immigration paperwork even if it was the last thing he did as honorary consul. It took Egil four months, one flight and two 16-hour round trips through the Canadian Rockies, driving between Calgary and Vernon, but 51 years and 10 months after arriving in Canada, Dag finally obtained his permanent residency card. Days later, Egil received Dag's emergency passport from the Norwegian embassy in Ottawa. And just like that, Dag had the paperwork required to get him to Norway and back.

I said goodbye to my pregnant wife, boarded a plane from Ottawa and flew four hours west to Calgary, where I rented a jeep and proceeded to drive eight more hours into British Columbia to collect Dag. He was wandering down the gravel road near the bus when I found him. He was excited at the prospect of returning to Norway, but he was also uneasy that he couldn't afford any of it.

"I don't know how to repay you for this," he said.

"You don't have to," I told him.

After he collected a few items from the bus (an extra set of clothes and a jacket that he stuffed inside a backpack that was duct-taped together), we began the long drive back to Calgary to catch a flight for Amsterdam and onward to Oslo.

For months I had been communicating with members of Dag's extended adoptive family, letting them know I would be travelling with him back to Norway to connect with family and to learn about his past. Not everyone had faith that I would actually materialize with Dag in Sigdal. As his cousin Gunhild Bakke, the 78-year-old matriarch of one line of the Skartum side of the family, told me during one of many phone calls in the lead-up to our arrival: "Dag has been gone so long, we did not think we would ever see him again. There will be many people here who will want to see him or to meet him."

I asked Gunhild one day whether she or anyone else in Georg or Helga's extended family had known anything about Dag's biological parents.

"Dag was always a mystery to us," she said. "Helga and Georg never told anyone where he came from. He just arrived one day and that was that." She said she had grown skeptical of the stories about Dag that had appeared over the years in the media and of those who told them. So much of what she had seen and read had failed to capture the story of the boy she had grown up with and the man she knew. "I hope you are different," she said.

I understood from Gunhild that many people in the village would be excited by Dag's return, but I did not expect that they would gather by the dozens to meet him when he arrived. Or that they would come from as far away as Denmark just for the opportunity to see him one last time.

Of all the people who had ever known him in Europe, none had been more taken by the prospect of seeing him again than Kari Jørgensen. I had found her number written in the back of one of Dag's journals and asked who she was. Kari was ten years younger than Dag. The daughter of Helga's youngest sister, Kari had known Dag for as long as she could remember. She spent her summers at Hovlandsmoen during the 1950s. She later worked as a doctor in Copenhagen but was now retired, divorced, recovering from a stroke and conscious of the limited time that she had left on the planet. She had fallen in love late in life with a retired Danish firefighter, and together they drove the 650 kilometres from Copenhagen to Oslo just to meet us at the airport.

We had no sooner cleared customs at Oslo's Gardermoen Airport when Kari spotted Dag and began moving fast toward him with arms open. She had loved him ever since they were children, when she had looked up to him as an older brother, knit him sweaters and watched in awe as he walked through the village on his hands with shopping bags dangling from his feet. Three years earlier, Kari had flown from her home in Copenhagen to Vernon to see him on his 75th birthday, because she was getting old and he was getting old and she worried that if she did not travel then, she might not get the chance to see him one last time before they both grew too old to travel. She had struggled with the goodbye on that trip, as had he, and as she prepared to leave him she asked him if he wanted to leave the bus behind and return with her to Europe. He told her then that he no longer believed he could live in an actual home, let alone a home in a European capital. Nor did he believe that he could be a good companion to anyone. "My home," he told her, "is alone on my trails."

SITTING IN THE back seat of Kari's new Mercedes, Dag looked out the window as we made our way along the hilly shorelines of the inland lakes that riddle the countryside between the capital and the valley of Sigdal. It was early afternoon when we arrived at a farm that had once belonged to Helga's eldest sister, Anna, but which had since been passed down to Anna's eldest son, Carl. Carl was a farmer and had lived the life that Dag had forsaken a long time ago. It was Carl who had come to Helga's aid near the end of her life, reclaiming Hovlandsmoen for his line of the family after Dag had forfeited his claim to the land. Carl had long since passed Hovlandsmoen down to his own son, Hans-Ole, and continued to work the fields and forests of his own childhood farm. Now Carl stood in the doorway of the home in which he had lived for 68 years and welcomed us inside.

Soon we were gathered around the dining table, eating a traditional Norwegian sour-cream porridge. I listened as Kari, Carl and his wife reminisced with Dag about things he thought he had forgotten. They spoke of Helga and of Georg and updated Dag on all aspects of the world he left behind. And they asked about the life he had made for himself in Canada. They had all seen the video of Dag on YouTube, but what they really wanted to know was what had happened to his family. Dag spoke of his children and his grandchildren as he always did, making it sound as if he had seen them just the other week. Then the talk turned to the reason for our trip.

"What is it you hope to find here?" Carl asked.

I told him I didn't really know, but that I had managed to track down Dag's adoption records and there was a file with Dag's name on it waiting for him in Oslo.

Carl's wife looked at me, curious. "This file in Oslo," she said. "How much will it tell you about his parents?"

"I don't know," I said.

"How much do you *want* to know?" she asked.

"As much as there is," Dag said.

We slept that night in the old house on Carl's farm. I could hear Dag rustling in the night, making his way out into the cold for a run. I lay in bed jet-lagged and groggy. It was just after dawn and the sun was piercing through the pines and spruce outside my window when I heard the front door open and close as Dag came back from his run. I gathered my notebooks and walked through the creaky house down to the dining room to meet him. Soon we were back in the Mercedes, driving toward Oslo to collect the file containing the only known records of Dag's adoption.

The Oslo office of the Norwegian Directorate for Children, Youth and Family Affairs is a generic, modern seven-storey office block that sits among other nondescript office blocks in a mixed commercial/industrial zone next to a major highway in the east end of the city. Dag eyed the building cautiously before we checked in with security and took a seat in a waiting area next to a coffee machine and a water cooler where countless other adults had sat before us. As we waited for a member of the Norwegian bureaucracy to come down an elevator with the secrets of Dag's existence, I had no idea what to expect, but I hoped that all our effort would be worth it.

When I first exchanged emails with a senior advisor at the directorate weeks earlier, she explained that Dag's file wasn't exactly complete. Documents seemed to be missing. Items that may have once contained photos of his parents had been either lost or destroyed or were, perhaps, still held in some of the regional archives that made up the larger Norwegian archival apparatus. There was no way of knowing what else might be out there without expending significantly more time and energy than anyone in the office could allot to one single case.

The elevator dinged and Bente Hoseth stepped out into the foyer and was soon shaking Dag's hand and telling him what he already knew: that he had come a long way and that she hoped what she was about to give him would be worth his trouble. "Everything we have is in this file," she said, handing him a white envelope. Dag thanked her and held it in his hand for a moment before opening it on his lap. Soon he was leafing through a seven-page packet. Hoseth took a seat beside us.

The first page was marked "Information about biological parents." "It is stated in the Central Adoption Register," Dag translated for my benefit as he read, "that Georg Johnsen Aabye and

Helga Aabye, born Skartum, were granted permission by the Ministry of Justice on Oct. 27, 1942, to adopt Erik, born in Oslo on May 15, 1941. At the same time, an authorization was given to change the child's name to Dag Skartum Aabye. Attached is a copy of the adoption case documents contained in our archive."

Dag looked up from the page. "I never knew I had a middle name," he said. Helga and Georg had given him the name of the old Skartum family farm, the original source of Helga's family's wealth. It was the name the Norse had given to Helga's ancestral farm for its resemblance to "a beautiful place."

He lifted another page and began to translate a typed letter that had been dictated by his biological mother. "The home of the Oslo health council's adoption office can obtain my son, Erik, born in Oslo on May 15, 1941. The adopter will raise the child as his own, and the undersigned agrees that the child is to be adopted. I agree that the adoption permit provides that the inheritance relationship between the adoptive child and his or her life heirs shall be as between real parents and their life heirs. . . . I declare that I will never demand to know where the child is going."

Dag read the date aloud—July 7, 1942—followed by the name scrawled in clean, swooping cursive—Hedvig Marie Hansen. He pressed his finger against her handwriting. "I was 15 months old when she signed this," he said.

The document bore the signatures of two other witnesses, both compliance officers from the city's health department.

Then Dag leafed through to another letter, this one from his biological father. He read the letter aloud. It was similar to the one signed by his mother. Then he came to the place where his father's name was spelled out.

"His name is different here," I said.

"What?" Dag asked.

I pointed to the name. "Here he is Johan Olav Nilsen. In the church book, he was Nielsen."

"That seems suspicious, doesn't it?" I asked. The directorate's official didn't say a thing. It seemed weird that Dag's father's name would be spelled two different ways on the only two documents we had ever seen about him. I had been using the spelling from the church book in all my archive searches. "Maybe that's why I couldn't find anything about him," I said. "It's possible I've been searching the wrong name." The letter from Dag's father was dated several weeks after the one signed by his mother. It bore no other signature, no witness, just an address for a building in the city's north end.

Dag turned to another page and began reading a letter from Georg and Helga Aabye to the justice department, pleading their case to adopt him. It was dated September 9, 1942. It was accompanied by a letter from a vicar in Sigdal vouching for the adoptive parents' capacity to care for a child. "I have known the farmer Georg Aabye and his wife, Helga, for several years," the vicar wrote. "They are very honest and law-abiding people. I have only one opinion—that it will be an advantage for any child to be adopted by such a couple."

The last document in the file was a receipt for 40 kroner, paid to the Oslo Health Board. It was the fee Helga and Georg had paid to formalize the adoption. Dag flipped through the papers front to back once more. Then he went back to the page with his mother's signature and held it for a while.

"This is the only time I've ever seen her handwriting," he said.

The directorate's advisor looked at him, apologized that she couldn't give him more, and then left him with the file.

WE GOT BACK to the car and sat inside for a few minutes. Neither of us was entirely sure what to make of what we had just read.

Then Dag spoke. "I wouldn't mind seeing where my mother lived."

I pulled out my phone and punched in the address for the old hotel that Hedvig had listed as her residence on the day of Dag's baptism. We pulled up to the red-brick structure, just off one of Oslo's busier pedestrian streets. Dag climbed out of the car and walked alone toward the building. When he reached its side, he ran his hand along the bricks and walked the perimeter of the four-storey multi-unit complex. Then he backed away from the building, reached into his pocket and pulled out an instant camera—the type you buy at a drug store. He wound the camera with his thumb and took a few photos. He would add them to one of his journals when he got back home.

We drove deeper into Oslo, toward the site of the orphanage where Dag had spent almost a year of his early life, just beyond the fortress walls of the Oslo Prison. Soon we were staring at a white stucco building that had stood in place for more than a hundred years. I read the sign outside the building: Åkeberg kindergarten.

"That's it," I said. "Dag, that's the orphanage."

A low fence encircled the building. Bicycles and strollers rested in tidy racks inside the fence. I slowed the car to a halt in front of the building.

"This is where your mother left you and where Georg and Helga picked you up," I said. I undid my seatbelt.

Dag stared out the window of the car. He watched as, just outside the gate, a father helped his son buckle up a bicycle helmet. Then the son took off on his tricycle through the gate and onto the old orphanage grounds.

I was about to open my door when Dag stopped me.

"It's okay," he said. "I've seen enough."

TWENTY-THREE

HEDVIG'S FATE

Young Norwegian girls and women who had relations with German soldiers or were suspected of having them were victims of undignified treatment. Our conclusion is that Norwegian authorities violated the fundamental principle that no citizen can be punished without trial or sentenced without law. For many, this was just a teenage love, for some, the love of their lives with an enemy soldier or an innocent flirt that left its mark for the rest of their lives. Today, in the name of the government, I want to offer my apologies.

—NORWEGIAN PRIME MINISTER ERNA SOLBERG, SPEAKING AT AN EVENT TO MARK THE 70TH ANNIVERSARY OF THE UN'S UNIVERSAL DECLARATION OF HUMAN RIGHTS, OCTOBER 17, 2018

Dag pulled his tuque over his head and stepped out into the darkness. I zipped up my jacket and followed. Six days had passed since we had driven to Oslo to pick up his adoption records. It was just after 5 a.m. Our feet crunched against the frost-covered ground as we made our way toward our rented Citroën.

Dag let out a deep breath as we walked. His breath hung in the air for a moment. He watched as it dispersed into the darkness. "I love this time of morning," he said.

I shivered as I unlocked the car and climbed into the driver's seat. Dag paced around in the darkness while I warmed up the vehicle. He was letting out pent-up energy in preparation for the 10-hour drive we were about to undertake. He seemed anxious, though he didn't vocalize it as we set out toward Sweden and Gothenburg and the place where his mother had worked and where she had died.

Dag climbed into the passenger seat. I turned on the high beams and started down the backcountry road that cut through Skartum. We had spent the previous five days with Dag's adoptive cousin Gunhild and her husband. Night in and night out, Gunhild's entire family, including her sons and daughter and grandchildren, had come to spend as much time as possible with Dag because they knew

Dag and the old house where he grew up in Hovlandsmoen. (Courtesy of the author)

that once he left they were unlikely to see him again. The reception had been similarly overwhelming all through Sigdal, especially after his presence in the valley made the front page of the local newspaper.

Dag peered out the window in the darkened valley as we snaked along the river, heading south toward Oslo and the sea. The farms rolled by on either side of us, just out of reach from our headlights, yet visible in the strong moonlight. Every white manor farmhouse and red wood barn we passed looked like it could be on a postcard. We were only 10 minutes into our journey when we passed Hovlandsmoen. A lone lamp shone through one of the upper windows. Dag kept his eyes fixed on his childhood home as we drove closer. We had been inside the manor days earlier, guests of honour at a meal hosted by its current owner, Dag's second cousin, Hans-Ole, son of Carl. Twenty guests had joined us that evening, including some who hadn't set foot inside the house since Helga died.

Nothing Dag had ever told me led me to believe that he recognized or understood the effect his departure had on the rest of his adoptive family. Certain members of the family had hardly spoken for 28 years, until they found themselves seated across from each other at the dinner in Dag's honour at Hovlandsmoen.

We had sat and eaten on fine china, and then, when the meal was over and the guests were mingling around the living room drinking coffee and finishing dessert, Hans-Ole's wife, Jeanette, took Dag and me aside to tell us about the things she found in the home shortly after they moved in.

"Helga had some beautiful pieces," she said, "but there were some scary things in this house." She described jars of pickled snakes and lizards under the staircase, tokens that had been brought back from Argentina.

Then she showed us a large hardcover book she had found under a thick layer of dust. She said it was the Aabyes' old guest book. Every dinner party was logged, every overnight guest, every family birthday. More than half the pages were still blank when she found it, so she had placed it on the coffee table to be used as her family's guest book too.

I flipped to the first entry. It was dated September 24, 1942. The message in Norwegian read: "Thank you so much for my visit and congratulations with Dag." I looked at the signature. I had seen it days earlier in Dag's adoption file. It had been on a letter from the Oslo Health Board to the justice department dated September 12, 1942. And here it was again.

Dag tried to decipher the name, but could not. Then he flipped to the next page in the guest book. That entry was dated October 28—the day after Helga and Georg had been granted permission to adopt. Dag read out the words: "Wishing you all the happiness with Dag."

I looked again at the book in his hands. It was leather-bound and several hundred pages long. "This wasn't originally the farm's guest book," I said. "This one begins with your arrival." Dag flipped through a few more pages. They were all filled with messages from the friends and family that Helga and Georg had invited to the farm in the first few days after his adoption. It wasn't until several days later that the messages started to refer to subjects other than Dag.

"I think this book was originally meant to tell the story of your life," I told him.

Dag looked to Jeanette.

"I had no idea," she said.

Dag read a few more passages, then handed the book back to me and sat alone with his thoughts. I was leafing through the book when one of Dag's childhood neighbours took me aside.

"I'm not sure how much he remembers about what he went through in this house," the neighbour told me. "They starved and tormented him. He would come over to our farm looking for milk or food because he wasn't getting any here. When he was four years old, his mother took him outside in the dark and left him to find his way to the outhouse and then back again to the door. He was terrified and when he got back to the house, screaming, she just said to him, 'There is nothing in the dark that isn't there in the light.'

"He was completely traumatized here as a child," the neighbour continued. "Helga treated him very badly."

"Why was that?" I asked.

She shook her head. "We never knew why," she said. "Some people thought maybe he was actually Georg's son and not hers. But none of us really knew for sure."

This revelation left me with more questions than answers. Why had Helga invited all her friends to welcome Dag to the farm on the day he was adopted? And why had she commissioned an oil painting of the young Dag that she kept on the wall long after he had run away? And why did she make a point of saving his cabin for him in the end?

It didn't make sense.

HOVLANDSMOEN DISAPPEARED ALONG with the moonlight in the rear-view mirror as Dag and I carried on out of the valley in silence.

The night was giving way to a grey morning by the time we reached the Swedish border and continued to drive through a sleet storm as we followed the coast toward Gothenburg. Sweden's second-largest city was teeming with mid-morning traffic when we arrived. Soon we were above the city, looking down on cruise ships and freighters as we crossed a steel bridge over the Göta River and followed the tramlines into the city's centre. We had come to see the place where Dag's mother spent the last 25 years of her life—where she lived after she gave him up for adoption, and where she died. She was buried in an unmarked grave near the city centre.

Our trip had coincided with an overdue reckoning by Norwegian society over its unfair treatment of the women who had had relationships with German soldiers during the war. Eight days before we set out for Gothenburg, the Norwegian prime minister issued a public apology to those women on behalf of the country—even though most were already dead. The apology was on both our minds as we found our way through the neighbourhood where Dag's mother had lived until the time of her death. The sleet had turned to heavy rain, which pelted the windshield as we drove slowly down a bumpy cobbled road lined by derelict buildings with boarded-up windows and doors hanging on busted hinges. I pulled the car over and read the number above the broken door on one of the most dilapidated buildings on the street.

"That's it," I said. "That's where she lived."

Dag unbuckled his seatbelt and stepped outside.

Dag's biological mother lived in a small apartment in this building in an old part of Gothenburg, Sweden. (Courtesy of the author)

"Do you want me to come with you?" I asked through the window as he stood on the street in the pouring rain.

"I don't know," he said.

A car honked. Dag raised his hand, then crossed the street, pushed through the broken door and vanished inside. I waited in the car for a few minutes before I hit the four-ways and followed him.

The building was rougher on the inside than it was on the outside. A pile of leaves, brought in by the wind, rested on the floor next to a staircase. The plaster walls were peeling and covered in mould. I walked up the stairs in search of Dag. I called out his name, but heard nothing. I kept climbing until I found him, standing by an open window that looked down into a parkette behind the building. He looked as if he was in shock.

"She must have walked these stairs countless times," he said. "I didn't expect her to feel so real."

WE DROVE ON toward the graveyard. The rain was falling harder as we pulled into the cemetery. A young woman in the office watched as we ran through the rain from our car. Soon she was looking through the cemetery records trying to locate the site of an unmarked grave.

"I don't believe your mother ever had a tombstone," she told Dag.

"Is that normal?" I asked.

"If there was no family to purchase a stone, then there would be no marker," the woman explained.

"A pauper's grave," Dag said.

She pulled out a map of the grounds and pointed to a space that had been used as a communal gravesite reserved for the poor. Dag watched and listened as the woman pointed through a window toward a grassy knoll with no monuments on it, not far from where we had parked.

"She's under that hill somewhere. I'm sorry I can't be any more precise for you."

We walked out into the rain, toward the knoll, until we were standing at the edge of the grass.

"I wonder if anyone else has ever come looking for her," Dag said. He took one step onto the grass and then stopped.

"I'm sorry there wasn't something more here to cling to," I said.

We ran back to the car through the pouring rain. For a moment we just sat inside, waiting for the car to heat up as rain pattered against the windshield. Dag was still looking out toward where his mother was buried. I reached into the back seat for an envelope and began searching the papers inside for the address where his mother had lived and worked when she first arrived from Norway. I punched it into my phone. Then I looked over at Dag, who was still staring out the window.

"Are you okay?" I asked. "We can just stay here for a bit if you want to."

"I understand," he said. "But I'm ready to go."

I slowly pulled out of the cemetery's parking lot and began navigating us toward our final destination.

Soon we were standing outside one of Gothenburg's posher restaurants. Dag stood on a rocky pier looking south over the Kattegat sea while I reviewed my notes about the 19th-century restaurant and inn where his mother had worked. The original building had been demolished in the years since, replaced by a modern edifice that carried the same name.

It was no longer raining. A cool mist rolled off the sea, dampening the shore. Dag looked at the restaurant in all its grandeur and the yachts moored just beyond the patio.

"This is a fancy place," I said.

"What was my mother doing here?" Dag asked.

"She worked as a dishwasher," I said.

"A dishwasher?"

"Yes," I said.

"Like me," Dag said. He took another few steps toward the shore, then just looked blankly out to sea. "You don't need to show me any more," he said. "You have given me more than you know."

TWENTY-FOUR

ALL WE LEAVE BEHIND

The only thing constant—is change.
—HERACLITUS, QUOTED IN DAG'S JOURNALS

Dag said goodbye to Sigdal just a few days later. I watched quietly as he hugged Gunhild and promised that he would come back to see her again soon. But it was clear, from the way she held his face before he left, that she knew this was their last goodbye.

And then we were gone, driving through a pre-dawn snowstorm on our way to the airport. It took us 18 hours and four flights to get back to Dag's lair on the other side of the planet. It was dark when our first flight took off out of Oslo and it was dark again when our last flight touched down in Kelowna. It was nearly midnight when I pulled yet another rented Chevy back up the gravel road toward a chain barrier that marked the end of the road and the start of one of the footpaths to Dag's bus.

We were back to where we had said our first goodbye years earlier. The very place where Dag had planted himself in my mind with his words: "I was born in captivity. It was nature that set me free." I had left him at that spot a dozen times over the years. I was used to watching the lamp on his forehead fade into the darkness of the forest. I always left him assuming that I might never see him again. Then I would begin the long journey across the country to my own home.

But this time, there was more finality to it than before. I knew it would be a long time before I would be able to make it back to see him again. My wife was five months pregnant with our first child, and I knew that my life was about to change significantly. It was hard to fathom when I would next be able to skip across the country to wander the wilderness with Dag. But more than just my own impending parenthood was weighing on my mind.

We had just spent 10 days surrounded by his childhood friends and family while searching for his biological parents. It was an intense experience for Dag, who had spent so much of the last

20 years of his life in relative seclusion. There were moments during the trip when I wondered why he would even want to come back with me to Canada. I reflected a few times on what his daughter had said to me on the phone before we set out for Norway. How she thought it might be better for him to stay there if he could. He didn't have much to come back to. But he had come back, and now I was depositing him on a dark trail into a dark forest with nothing much waiting for him other than a rotting bus filled with garbage and mouldy books and photos and journals. As we rolled toward our final destination, I couldn't help but feel that I had failed Dag in some way. I had led him out of this place on a journey of discovery, and now we were back at the beginning and it wasn't entirely clear to me how much any of it had been worth.

I put the car in park and turned off the engine while he rummaged through his bag searching for his headlamp.

"I'm sorry there wasn't more for you out there," I said.

He asked me what I meant.

"I don't know," I said.

He stopped rummaging for a moment. "I see," he said. "You wanted to give my story a happy ending."

I looked at him, dumbstruck.

He pointed at his head and then at his chest. "Happiness is in here," he said. Then he pointed out the window. "It's up to us to bring it out there. We're not going to just find it somewhere."

He flipped on his headlamp and picked his backpack up from the floor of the car, then he looked at me again and asked: "What will you do when you get home to your family?"

I smiled. "I guess I'll get on with my life," I said. "And start writing up yours."

"Aw," he said. "You've made enough sense of my life?"

"I don't know if that's possible," I said.

"Make sure you take the time to make sense of yours too."

I laughed and looked out into the darkness.

"Are you going to be okay?" I said.

"I will always be okay," he said. Then he stepped out into the night and leaned down before he shut the door. "I'm just going to keep pushing as hard as I can until the end," he said.

I turned on the headlights to help him find his way. "Take care of yourself," I said.

He looked at the light illuminating the forest, then back at me. "There is nothing in the darkness that isn't there in the light," he said.

Then he started making his way into the bush.

I watched until the light from his headlamp faded out of sight.

Two days later, I was still filtering back into my own existence at home when my phone rang. It was my mother. She had been fascinated by Dag ever since I first told her about him. She wanted to know whether he and I had found what we were looking for.

I told her that I thought he had found what he wanted but that I was still trying to figure a few things out. I told her about his biological mother's grave and what little I had managed to piece together from her life. So much of her life and what had transpired between them remained a mystery that I didn't believe I, or anyone else, could help him solve.

She asked how he had been when I left him and I shared with her what he had said about pushing as hard as he could until the end. She was inspired by his outlook. "I think it's what keeps him alive," I said. Then I asked how she was doing. She told me she had been having trouble finding her words and how it bothered her enough that she went to her doctor to get some tests. She was still waiting for the results.

We said goodbye and I went back to my desk and continued digging through online archives and databases for anything that might fill in the gaps in my understanding of who Dag's mother had been. It hadn't occurred to me yet that, with his parting words, Dag had been trying to give me some important advice, or that by laughing it off I had failed to hear him.

But that would set in shortly, when my phone rang with another call from my mother. She had received the results of her recent scan. The cancer she had been fighting in her breast had spread to her brain. Within weeks she would undergo emergency brain surgery to remove two tumours. But the cancer continued to spread, to her lungs, her abdomen and once more to her brain. She knew she didn't have long, but she was driven to hold on long enough to meet my first-born daughter. The five months between the time she learned she had terminal cancer and her death were gruelling—mentally, emotionally and physically. Through it all, she was guided by her spirituality and her own determination.

As the disease spread through her body, she lost her capacity to read and asked instead that I read to her. All she wanted to hear, though, were the words I was trying to write about Dag. Night after night I would recite to her pages of the old man's life, and when I ran out of pages I tried to fill in the blanks as best I could in conversation by her bedside. "I don't really know how it ends," I confessed. "Or what's the strongest part." I told her how I thought there was something universal to be learned from the story of an old man who had survived for years alone in the forest by pushing the physical limitations of his own decline. But I was still struggling to reconcile some of the other stories of Dag's life, especially the one of the orphaned child who was adopted into a family in which he never seemed to belong and who alienated himself from the family he had built as an adult.

"His philosophy is the strongest part," she said. Then she repeated some of his words back to me. "Time matters most when time is running out."

My mother had found meaning in those words as she progressively lost the ability to walk, laugh, speak and, eventually, eat. On rare occasions when she was well enough to get out of bed and into a wheelchair, she would ask to be taken to the physiotherapy room in her palliative ward, where she would work with nurses on mobility and strength. Each time she worked with a nurse to do something as simple as gripping a rubber ball, pushing her hands together or rotating her ankle, she found it frustrating and painful. But she continued to do it, knowing that if she didn't do so now, she might never do so again.

Throughout the later stages of her illness, as I sat by her bedside, holding her hand and reading to her, my phone would periodically ring from an unknown number. If my mother was awake I would tell her it was Dag and she would nod and I would step out of the room. Somewhere along the way he had stopped calling just to check in and begun calling to see if I was okay. "Cherish what you have right now," he said on one such call, "because one day it will be gone and you don't want to look back with any regrets." I thanked him for the advice and went back to my mother's bedside.

Then, as winter gave way to spring and my wife went into labour, I walked away from the palliative wing of one hospital and into the maternity ward of another. Hours before my daughter was born, as I slumped in a hospital chair next to my wife, Dag called. I ducked out of the room and answered the phone. He was standing in a Walmart parking lot—the same one he had called me from many times—as snow accumulated all around him, snow that would no doubt make it that much more difficult to get back to his bus. And yet there he was, listening as I told him what was transpiring in my life. I told him that I was just hours away from becoming a father and days away from losing my mother.

"We are never ready to lose a parent," he said. "You only have one mom. And your mom is the most important person in your life." Then he added something else that I thought of often in the days that followed: "If nothing changes after you've had a child, then you're not doing it right."

I thanked him for that and told him I would think about what he had just said.

"Enjoy the time you have for what it is," he said.

I SPENT THE days after my mother's death wandering my house without reason or purpose. Every time I sat down to write more of Dag's story I began reliving memories of reading and writing pages about his life while sitting in a palliative ward. The trauma lingered for months. I don't know how many times my phone rang from an unknown number during that time. Or how many messages Dag left on my phone. I appreciated every one of them. His friendship and his story still meant something to me, but I no longer knew why anything I had been doing before my daughter's birth or my mother's death mattered.

It was an unexpected email from an unlikely source that helped remind me what I had been working on and why. The email was a delayed response from an archivist in Oslo who was replying to an inquiry I sent shortly after returning from Norway. I had contacted the archives with questions about the children's home Dag had been adopted from. It wasn't one of the 12 Lebensborn facilities that had been set up in the country, but I wanted to know if there was any evidence that

Lebensborn children had lived within its walls. I also had questions about the hotel Dag's mother had listed as her place of residence when she had relinquished her rights to her son.

Though both Dag and I had separately been told that the hotel she called home was a hangout for Nazi soldiers and officers during the war, I had found no archival connection between the Lebensborn and the Åkeberg children's home. Nor had I found any official documentation linking Dag to the Lebensborn. The more I dug into it, the more I realized that Dag's own understanding of his origins had been shaped by the words shouted in anger at him by Helga about his biological mother. The fact that his adoptive parents had been Nazi sympathizers, that his biological mother had fled Norway immediately after the war, that someone somewhere had told him his father was a U-boat officer, that his adoptive parents had fled to Argentina—it all pointed toward the conclusion that Dag was either a Lebensborn child or had been fathered by a German in Norway during the war.

Then I opened the email from the Oslo archivist, and suddenly my understanding of why Dag's mother had given him up was completely overwritten.

The archivist wrote that the Åkeberg children's home "was purchased in 1921 by the Oslo

Circuit of the National Association for Tuberculosis and after the redevelopment was made available to the municipality as a home for tuberculosis-endangered infants."

I posed a follow-up question to the archivist: "Does this mean that a child who was in that home during that time was there because their parents had been sick with tuberculosis?"

"Yes," came the response. "Due to the need for such a home for children up to 5–6 years old, the home was expanded in 1930, and could accommodate 70 children. In the 1940 municipal textbook, it states that 'the home is scheduled to excavate a temporary home for healthy infants from homes where the mother or one of the family's other permanent members suffers from open-label infectious tuberculosis.'"

I looked away from my laptop and toward the pile of Dag's old journals resting by my desk. Then to the pile of research about his parents. Suddenly Dag's adoption took on a whole other meaning.

Days later, another email arrived, this one from the German Federal Archives. They had searched the records of the Kriegsmarine, the Wehrmacht and the Luftwaffe and found no reference to a soldier by the name of either Johan Olav Nielsen or Nilsen.

Weeks passed before Dag called me next, and

I told him that I had new information about his parentage to share with him.

"I think your parents gave you up because one or both of them were sick," I told him.

"What do you mean?" he asked.

"The orphanage you were adopted from was specifically set up for children whose parents were suffering from tuberculosis."

Then I told him that the Germans didn't appear to have any record of his father.

"But my father was a German soldier," Dag said.

"I'm not so sure of that anymore," I said.

"Then who was he?" Dag asked.

TWENTY-FIVE

MESSAGE IN A BOTTLE

*Of all the ways you can limit yourself, your
own self-definition is the most powerful.*
—ANONYMOUS QUOTE IN DAG'S JOURNALS

Dag pressed a plastic vial to his mouth and spat. Then he licked his lips, held the vial toward me and asked, "Is that enough?"

I checked the instructions on the Ancestry-DNA testing kit. "I think you need to spit out a little bit more," I said. He put the vial back to his mouth and spat again, then handed it back to me. I flipped the cap down onto the vial, turned it upside down and let the stabilizer mix with his saliva to preserve his genetic code for the long trip to a lab in Ireland.

"Do you think it will work?" he asked.

I put the little vial inside a shipping box with return postage. "I hope so," I said.

"And then if I have any siblings or cousins you will be able to find them?" he asked.

"That's the idea," I said. "We send this to Ireland, where they analyze your genetic code to see if it matches up with others in their database." I reached into the back seat of the car and pulled out another package, this one from 23andMe. "This one is a bit different," I said. "It uses a different database and gives a bit more information on your health and genetic history—like how far back your personal DNA line has been in Norway and how it got there and from where. They trace markers in your DNA back hundreds of generations, and in many cases they can track you back to a certain man or woman who migrated out of Africa thousands of years ago."

Dag opened the second vial, spat inside and handed it back for me to stabilize and seal.

It was August 2019. Eight months had passed since our trip to Norway. Eight months since Dag had stood in the grass of a Gothenburg cemetery, looked at the general vicinity of his mother's unmarked grave and wondered whether anyone else had ever come looking for her.

"There's always a chance that this won't prove

anything," I said. "But I think it's the only way you're ever going to find out anything about your father."

"Then it's worth it."

I HADN'T THOUGHT of trying to trace Dag's genealogy through his DNA when he first explained the mystery that surrounded his parentage. I wasn't entirely convinced that it was an even trade to give a company your DNA—forever—in exchange for personal data that they were collecting from a cross-section of humanity. I wasn't sure how comfortable Dag would be with it either. But I had run out of ideas about where to search for information about his father, and I couldn't think of any other ways to locate distant relatives on either side of his family who might know anything about his parents. I felt I had exhausted every other option. If he really wanted to know if he had any other family, he would have to spit into a bottle and entrust some internet company with his genetic code. When he agreed, I purchased two DNA testing kits so that he could see what the lab technicians could decipher from the approximately 700,000 single nucleotide polymorphisms, tiny variations in his genome, contained in one sample of his saliva.

There were pros and cons to adding his code to these databases, which I explained to Dag.

He had read several news stories over the years of people taking such tests and finding out that their parents weren't who they said they were. He said he was open to trying it because he understood that cross-referencing the contents of his saliva with the contents of hundreds of thousands of other people's saliva was perhaps the best possible chance to uncover, among other things, the identity of his father.

"There's one other thing you should be aware of before we go down this path," I said.

He turned his head toward me.

"There's a chance," I explained, "that if your son in Chile has also taken one of these tests, he could find you in one of these databases. I don't know if that's a risk or just a reality."

Dag looked at the packages in his hands and then out the window toward the lookout where he had spent countless days alone.

"You don't have to do this," I said.

He handed the packages back to me. "Let's see what they find," he said.

It was an excruciatingly hot Monday in August when Dag handed me the vials with his saliva. We sat in a rental car on the side of the Okanagan Highway looking up at the mountainside that had been his training ground for 20 years. It was the first time I had seen him since losing my mother and becoming a father myself. He'd had a couple more falls during the intervening months and was barely able to use his right arm for anything because of his dislocated shoulder. Despite the complications, he was getting in more training hours than ever and was on pace to break his own record for hours spent running in a single year. He was eager to get back to his old hilltop perch, the one where he had taken Derek, Myles and me on our first encounter, but he hadn't been able to get to it on his own in years. The perch was nowhere near his bus and infinitely more difficult to access. I wasn't sure that he would still be able to make it back to the top of the hill. It required a three-hour hike up from the highway through the animal-bone field and over the rugged mountainside by way of an abandoned logging road. Three years had passed since he last managed to hike into that camp and, looking at him, I wasn't convinced he would still be able to navigate the steep inclines. But he insisted that he wanted to try.

We drove down the highway to the gravel quarry near the boneyard. I pulled off the road and stashed the car next to a sage bush, grabbed my backpack filled with water and followed Dag up a steep sand dune and beyond the field filled with rotting deer carcasses until we reached a barbed wire fence. I watched as Dag used his good arm to push up a line of fence, creating a gap just big enough for him to squeeze through without catching his bare skin on the wire. I tried to do the same but hooked my arm on a rusted barb and cut a three-inch gash along the side of my bicep. Blood pumped through my shirt. The cut was painful and deep. Dag looked at my wound and asked if I wanted to go back. I too looked at the blood pouring out of my arm. I wrapped a bandana around the wound to stop the bleeding and signalled that I was ready to keep going.

For two hours we continued upwards, climbing the equivalent of a 77-storey building as we navigated over the stream that had once served as his clothes wash, past the old logging road and up the steep incline that led to the lookout. I wrapped my bloody arm around tree trunks and grasped at fallen branches to help pull myself up over the steepest parts of the trek. Dag set the pace. He had lost strength and mobility in his right arm, so he stabilized himself with a stick that he picked up from the ground. He kept it firmly gripped in his left hand and speared it into the earth whenever he needed extra traction or leverage. Then he would pull his body weight forward as he climbed. He paused at the top of one particularly difficult part of the trail that was so steep the pebbles and earth dislodged by our feet tumbled down the slope out of sight.

"I don't know how you're managing to do this with one arm," I told him.

He looked at my own bloody arm and didn't say a thing. It was early afternoon and the full heat of the day was upon us by the time we reached the deceiving wall of cedars that concealed his camp from the world. It didn't take long to realize that someone or something had ransacked the camp. The old tent structure that had been his living quarters was completely shredded, and the foam mattress ripped into countless pieces that were spread out all over the forest floor. The gas can for Dag's chainsaw looked like it had been dragged through the forest. His coffee mug had been smashed and cans of food looked like they had been beaten against a rock, as did the Rubbermaid container that had once stored most of his belongings. Pretty much everything that Dag had left behind had been destroyed or torn apart.

"What happened to this place?" I asked.

"Bears must have gotten to it," Dag said.

I looked around at the devastation. "They went through everything," I said.

"I can't just leave it like this," he replied.

"There's too much for you and me to carry down to the road," I said.

He wandered aimlessly through the site, picking up random pieces of his former camp and placing them in a pile next to the firepit. I watched for a bit as he tried to organize the things he had brought to this space so that they did not leave such a lasting scar on the hillside. Then I reached down into the earth and brushed off some of the old books that had become so bleached by the sun the words had been all but erased from the covers. I was reminded of his eclectic reading tastes. As I looked over the remnants of his camp, it struck me that what had happened here was destined to happen to his bus too. That someday soon he would die and the bears would move in and ransack the little lair he had created for himself.

Dag dropped a handful of empty cans next to the firepit. "I have to come back and bury all of this," he said.

"I don't think you're going to be able to rebuild what was here," I said.

"It will be better," he said, "when all of this is gone."

I LEFT DAG at the end of that trip and returned home with the two vials of his saliva. I dropped them in the mail and forgot about them for weeks. Then one day a message appeared in my inbox from a woman in Hawaii. She reached out via AncestryDNA. She had been using the site for four years, trying to build her family tree, when suddenly Dag's name popped into her tree. The system had concluded that Dag's DNA and her DNA had enough similarities to make them second cousins. She said she could see from her own tree that Dag was related to her through either her father, Ernest Earl Jansen, a US naval vet who had been born in Wisconsin in 1925 and died in 1980 on the outskirts of Chicago, or her paternal grandmother, Borghild Astrid Nilsen, who had been born in Oslo in 1886 and died in 1926 in a small town in upstate Wisconsin shortly after the birth of her third child. The woman asked if I knew who Dag's parents were and left a link to her family tree.

I opened up her tree on my computer and began trying to find the genetic link. It didn't take long. There on this Hawaiian stranger's Ancestry.com page was a photo of a woman who turned out to be Dag's biological aunt—Borghild Astrid Nilsen. Though Borghild had died 96 years earlier, she shared the same last name as Dag's biological father on his adoption paper and was Dag's father's eldest sister. Buried within this stranger's family tree was evidence that Dag's father had been born in Oslo too.

The sample of genetic code in Dag's saliva proved that he was not German at all. Johan Olav Nilsen was a Norwegian. Whoever told Dag that the name was cover for a Nazi soldier had either lied to him or been misinformed.

I clicked on Borghild's profile and began to read. Born in Oslo, she had spent her early childhood living with her family near the same parish church where Dag had been baptized. A handful of documents chronicled her life: a baptismal certificate, some immigration papers, a census or two, a marriage certificate and a death certificate. In a handwritten census form from 1900, I found a listing for her then nine-year-old brother, Johan Olav. I cross-referenced the census information with what was in the old church book. There was a small discrepancy. On the census Dag's father's birth year was listed as 1891. In the church book it was 1892. It was a common error, but it explained why I hadn't been able to find him anywhere.

With a simple spit of saliva, everything Dag had been led to believe about his parentage since he was a boy was disproven. The tiny mutations in his DNA sample had matched up with the tiny mutations in the DNA sample that had come from his cousin in Hawaii. Now I could see, in her family tree, that Dag's father had been born on March 27, 1891, the fourth of six children who grew up in a small home in central Oslo. Soon I was engaging with Dag's cousin, learning what had happened to Dag's grandparents as well as his aunts and uncles. He had first and second cousins in Wisconsin, Boston, New York and northern Indiana. I gathered what information there was and built a file to share with Dag the next time I saw him. I pored over each of his biological relatives on the site. There were dozens on his father's side, though none were close enough to offer any insights into the life of Johan Olav Nilsen. All Dag's cousin and I could figure out was that he had been living with his parents at the time of the 1900 and 1910 censuses, and then he seemed to disappear. The next official document that I could find with his name on it was Dag's baptism certificate, dated 1941. By then Johan was 50 years old and gave no address. None of his surviving extended family had any idea what had happened to him. No one knew when he died or where he was buried. No one knew what he had done for a living.

It would be weeks before I was able to reach Dag again to tell him what I had learned from his DNA. It seemed a lot to unpack. He had gone through the majority of his life believing he was the product of a Nazi eugenics experiment. I had my doubts that at 78 years old, learning the truth about his origins would change him at all.

I was still waiting to hear from Dag when I received an email from 23andMe. Their database was linking him to many of the same individuals he had been linked to through Ancestry. His lab results pegged him as 90.3 per cent Scandinavian, and although they hadn't identified any direct relatives, they had traced his DNA through his mother's side all the way back to a single woman who had lived in eastern Africa some 150,000 years ago. His mother's line had left Africa and crossed the Red Sea around 60,000 years ago, and lived around the Mediterranean and in the Middle East through to the end of the last Ice Age before moving toward Iberia and following the Atlantic coast north toward the British Isles, ultimately moving on to Scandinavia around 4,000 BC. It was all very macro and historic, but suddenly Dag's mother had a backstory, albeit a longer one than Dag had ever searched for.

The strains of DNA from Dag's father told a similar story. Like more than 10 per cent of Europeans in Scandinavia, the Balkans and eastern Europe, Dag was the descendant of some of the first *Homo sapiens* to have inhabited Europe around 30,000 years ago—hunter-gatherers who migrated out of Africa, north through the

Middle East, up through Germany and into the Baltic region before being pushed south again by the advancing Ice Age. Traces of Dag's ancestry could be found all through modern-day Spain, Italy and the Balkans. When the ice subsided roughly 12,000 years ago, a subset of Dag's ancestors made their way back into what became Denmark and parts of Sweden and Norway. These were the ones who drew on the sides of Nordic caves, hunted elk and deer with bows and arrows and buried their skis in peat bogs to preserve them through the summer months. The unknown knowns buried within the mutations in Dag's saliva were fascinating and revealing.

I'D HAD THE results of Dag's DNA tests for nearly a month before I heard from him again. As soon as he called me I told him that I thought he deserved to know the truth: that he was never the product of a dark secret or a distant war. Afterwards, I made plans to meet him at a set time on a set date at a set place on the gravel road near the bus. It was late November 2019 when I touched back down in Kelowna and climbed into another rental car. A fresh layer of snow was falling as I snaked my way through the Okanagan Valley before veering west up Silver Star Mountain Road and then north again along the gravel road that led toward Dag's bus. I drove slowly, a binder full of papers in the passenger seat, including a printout of his genealogical tree and the correspondence I'd had with distant relatives he didn't yet know existed. I had brought him everything I had because I wasn't sure when or if I would get back to see him again. He was falling and hurting himself more and more as the years wore on, but he showed no sign of easing up on the trails. He'd had yet another run-in with a black bear just weeks earlier. He had scared both himself and the bear when he jumped off the trail and fell chest first into a stump and knocked himself out. The bear was gone by the time he came to. Dag had struggled to breathe as he staggered back to the bus, only to roll onto his mattress, close his eyes and work through the pain.

The snow was falling in thick, wet clumps as I stopped the car next to our predetermined meeting place. I checked the clock on the car's dash—I was an hour late. I could see from the tracks on the road that Dag had already been here. He had paced back and forth along the road in the cold, then he seemed to have gone back into the forest. I sat and waited in the car, watching the snow accumulate on the windshield. I assumed he was running to warm himself up. I knew he would come back, I just didn't know when. An hour passed. The snow was getting thicker.

Then I saw him through the rear-view mirror, a spindly figure cutting through the trees, a bundle over his shoulder and a canvas bag swaying back and forth behind his head. I got out of the car and waved.

He carried the bag all the way to my car, then placed it down in the snow between us. "I brought these for you," he said.

I reached inside the bag. It was filled with more of his journals. I pulled out the one on top and flipped it open. Inside there was a five-year-old photo of the two of us in Jasper, from when I had driven him part of the way home after he ran his last Death Race. He had laminated the photo with Scotch tape and stuck it in his journal.

"I hope these are helpful to what you're doing," he said. "They have been invaluable to me."

"Thank you," I said.

I reached into the passenger seat and pulled out the binder I had prepared for him. "I brought you a bunch of information from your DNA test results," I said.

He looked at the binder in my hand, then asked: "Did I have any brothers or sisters?"

I shook my head.

"That's okay," he said.

"I have a lot to tell you," I said.

"I know a long trail," he said. "We can talk on the way."

We climbed into the car and I started driving, following Dag's directions out of the snow and into the valley, then north toward the base of a 600-metre cliff with a 15-kilometre trail that wound its way around the cliff wall and up to its peak. It was a 40-minute journey by car to the base of the cliff, and as we cut through the valley I told him everything I had learned from his DNA. About his parents, his grandparents—his lineage.

He listened quietly while looking at the road ahead, and I wondered if any of it really changed anything. There was no way of knowing how much of his life had been shaped by someone else's lie or mistake. But he had never let that bother him, and I was slowly beginning to understand why.

"I guess when you believe something long enough it becomes its own sort of truth," I said. "Even if it's really the unknown."

"What we know and what we believe are only part of what we understand," he said. Then he added: "In the end we have to live in the present, not the past."

We sat in silence for a while. Then I made one final turn toward the base of the cliff and slowed the car to a stop. "End of the road," I said.

"No," he replied. "It's just the start of the path."

Dag walks along the top of the Enderby Cliffs.
(Courtesy of the author)

EPILOGUE

THE LAST PLATEAU

But I have promises to keep,
And miles to go before I sleep

—ROBERT FROST, QUOTED IN DAG'S JOURNALS

For several months after that visit, Dag continued to call me every few weeks from a payphone. Despite the geographic distance between us, I remained one of his most frequent contacts. He closed out 2019 with more than 1,100 hours logged on his trails, averaging nearly three hours of running each day despite accumulating more and more injuries. He went into 2020 with the goal of breaking his all-time record for hours spent running every month of the year.

Then, as the COVID-19 pandemic hit and the world shut down, his calls became more infrequent. He was still out there, though, running day or night and living his life of relative solitude in the bus. He would descend the mountain and run into the city for food and supplies and find it locked down and abandoned. He was aware of what was going on from the news he consumed on the radio, but living on the outskirts of society, it felt to him like the pandemic was happening to people living on another planet. It didn't really have an impact on his life until the payphones he used were taken out of service, and though he wasn't entirely sure why, he assumed it was another public health precaution.

I heard from him only a handful of times after the pandemic set in. Spring turned to summer and summer to fall and suddenly it was October 31, 2020, and my phone was buzzing with a message from his youngest daughter. She said Dag had fallen again, and this time he had hurt himself badly. Someone had taken him to the hospital, and the doctors believed he had a fractured hip. But he had left the hospital and wasn't going back and now the doctors were searching for him and she didn't know where he was or where to look. My mind went to what he had once told me—that when the time came, he would just lie down in the forest and die. It would be days before I learned what really happened.

The snow had come early that October. Dag had been carrying a bag of food on his back as he made his way up the same gravel road where I had so often dropped him and said goodbye. He was alone when he lost his balance, slipped on some snow and fell to the ground, landing squarely on his hip. He didn't realize he was hurt until he tried to stand up. The pain in his hip brought him back down to the ground, this time falling on his side. For a moment he just lay in the snow, wincing. There was no way to call for help, and no way to get back on his feet either, so he crawled into the forest and continued to crawl up the hill to his bus. The wood stove inside had gone cold by the time he finally made it home.

He rebuilt the fire with the wood he had inside, then dragged his body into bed, closed his eyes and drifted away. When he woke again the fire was out and the bus was cold. He stepped out of bed, only to collapse on the floor. He crawled back to the woodpile, rebuilt the fire and sat by the stove to warm up. For two days he didn't leave the bus. The days were long, the nights cold. Then he ran out of wood to burn. He took some rope and his ski poles to use as crutches and left the bus. He was three hours into the process of trying to drag a stack of wood uphill and into the bus when a local resident who was out walking in the forest caught a glimpse of him struggling and took him to the hospital. The doctors said he had likely broken his hip, but Dag insisted that he was simply bruised. They gave him some real crutches so that he could stand up straight. He used them to walk out of the hospital.

He was still recovering from that fall six weeks later when I finally saw him again. He was back on his feet, walking his trails and preparing, as best he could, for the long winter ahead. He was moving slower than usual on a snow-covered road, making his way down to the city for some supplies, when I came upon him. I climbed out of the car to greet him, and we drove into town, picked up some cans of food, a couple of matchboxes and extra batteries for his headlamp. Before we headed back up to the bus he asked me if I wanted to go for one more hike. He said that down in the valley there was an abandoned rail line that snaked around a lake, not far from the home he once owned with Tony when he was a family man. He said the trail was long and winding and beautiful and that it would be nice to share it with a friend. Soon we were walking that old rail line, talking about his training and the endless kilometres he hoped to cover after he turned 80.

"I've written your story," I told him.

He slowed his pace and looked at me. "How does it end?" he asked.

"You tell me," I said.

He looked down at the pebbles beneath his feet, then back at me. "Leave me on a trail like this," he said. "Moving forward."

ACKNOWLEDGEMENTS

I didn't really know what I was getting into when I started writing this book. The journey from inception to completion has been long, but it was never lonely. I owe more thanks than I could ever cram into a few pages here. Thank you, first and foremost, to my wife, Corina, who lifted me up several times while I was working on this text and encouraged me to keep with it to the end. I don't know how many mornings you drove me to the airport in the dark so that I could fly away to meet with Dag. To my daughter, Mischa, who sat on my lap and on my shoulders as I worked through the early drafts of this text. And to my son, Niko, who is resting by my side as I write these final words. I remain grateful as well to my parents. To my father, who taught me that sometimes the search for meaning requires a backward glance. And to my mother, who helped me to visualize this book even though she herself was never able to see it.

ACKNOWLEDGEMENTS

Thank you to my tireless agent, Rick Broadhead. Your friendship means a lot to me. Thank you to the entire team at HarperCollins Canada for giving me the space and the time to recover when my life flipped upside down midway through the writing process. I remain grateful to Kate Cassaday, who took a chance on this story after hearing me talk about this fascinating guy I had met who lived in a bus on the side of a mountain. Thank you to Janice Zawerbny, who helped to focus the project when I was lost in the middle of it, and to Jim Gifford, who helped me to carry the book to the finish. Your editorial guidance was key to helping me form this text into what it is. And to Shaun Oakey for carefully copy-editing these pages and Natalie Meditsky for keeping us on schedule. Thank you also to the Ontario Arts Council for granting additional financial support to write this story through the Recommender Grants for Writers program, and to the Faculty of Public Affairs at Carleton University for assisting with the costs associated with fact-checking this text.

Many thanks to Myles McCutcheon for introducing me to Dag Aabye back in 2015. And to Derek Frankowski, with whom I started this journey.

To the Whistler Museum, the National Archives of Norway and the National Archives of

ACKNOWLEDGEMENTS

Sweden for their help in piecing together the disparate strands of information out of which I was able to build Dag's backstory. To Tina Knezevic, who helped fact-check large portions of this text, and to Egil Bjørnsen, the former Norwegian honorary consul, as well as the Royal Norwegian Embassy in Ottawa, and Dirk Sigalet back in Vernon, who were each instrumental in helping Dag to get back to Norway. To all of Dag's friends in Canada and in Norway who spoke with me for this project and helped me to better understand the remarkable life of the man at the centre of this book. And to all of Dag's family—near and far in Canada and in Norway.

And to Dag. I will remember your wisdom and friendship for the rest of my life, especially some of the parting words you gave to me the last time we met. "Find inspiration, find substance. Remember that it's always today."